MONEYLESS SOCIETY

MONEYLESS SOCIETY

THE NEXT ECONOMIC EVOLUTION

MATTHEW HOLTEN

CLEARSIGHT
BOOKS
Raleigh, North Carolina

ISBN hardback: 978-1-945209-33-8
ISBN paperback: 978-1-945209-34-5
ISBN ebook: 978-1-945209-35-2

Library of Congress Control Number: 2022917672

Published by Clear Sight Books, Raleigh, North Carolina
Cover design by Patricia Saxton

*To my mother, Kimberly, whose pain was unbearable,
but whose love guided me through the years.*

To my daughter, Lauren, and my son, Theo.

And to all who will inherit the earth when we are gone.

TABLE OF CONTENTS

INTRODUCTION

Having heard all of this you may choose to look the other way
but you can never say again that you did not know.

WILLIAM WILBERFORCE

Humans must change, in numerous ways, and fast. If we want to survive as a species, we have no choice. There is no real debate anymore as to whether we are destroying our world and, therefore, ourselves along with it. The increasing frequency and intensity of natural disasters in recent memory is alarming, to put it mildly. In 2020, California *doubled* its already record-breaking wildfire statistics from 2018, scorching more than 4 million acres[1]—over 4 percent of the state's total land. Greenland's ice loss has been so significant in recent years that it has caused a decrease in the gravitational field in the area.[2] The Great Barrier Reef—the only living structure that can be spotted from space—has now lost half its corals.[3] The sixth mass-extinction event[4] is at our doorstep, and most of us go about our day-to-day business as if we could not be any less concerned with the matter.

All these effects have come about in the last sixty years—even after we were warned, numerous times, that we were on a collision course with what might arguably be the worst disaster we could possibly imagine. Even many pro-business conservatives seem to exude a sense of unease that we may indeed be treading down a path from which we might not be able to return. The tide is inevitably shifting in favor of ecological stewardship and cooperation, although the pace is far too slow to produce real and lasting effects.

Add to the matter that for many people inequality and lack of resources are at levels that are starting to destabilize many regions. If the world's ten richest men lost 99.99 percent of their fortunes, their wealth would still surpass that of 99 percent of the world's population.[5] Scientists are warning of a "perfect storm" of events, culminating in the collapse of human civilization in the coming decades, as now being nearly unavoidable. Sweeping social and economic restructuring to curtail our society's vast inequality and destructive tendencies seems inevitable in the years to come, lest we continue to our own peril. Lurking on the horizon are existential threats for which we have no comparison in modern history. Yet as abundantly clear as so many of these things are, humans as a species are agonizingly slow to act.

THE MONETARY SYSTEM IS THE CORE PROBLEM

The main and most pressing reason for our inaction is the fact that the foundation of our society rests upon a system that incentivizes actions in direct opposition to our planet's and our own well-being: the monetary system and the social and economic structure it upholds.

The monetary system is so embedded in our culture that it

affects literally everything else. I would argue that it is by far the most significant single root cause and the largest contributing factor to nearly all our woes. Manufactured scarcity and pursuit of profit have sucked out of society the sense of community and compassion that has been essential to our survival and well-being for countless generations.

Yes, money is a tool as well as a system, and it can be used for better or worse. However, money is a tool that produces numerous unintended and undesired side effects, and would therefore be better off being retired. Money simply cannot solve the problems we currently face, because some of its inherent characteristics are contradictory to the solutions we need, and it has, in fact, created many of these problems in the first place. Because of the all-encompassing nature of capitalism and the monetary system, if we cannot bring ourselves to let go of our profit-oriented, consumer-driven culture, it is unlikely that we will be able to solve the problems these systems have created.

MOST OF US ARE AT A LOSS WHAT TO DO ABOUT IT

Most people know, on some level, that our social and economic systems need a massive overhaul, but they do not have a good grasp of why or of the best course of action. Most people are not exactly sure why capitalism is not compatible with life on this planet in the long term, or how the systems and structures our ancestors devised long ago created our current situation; therefore, they don't know what needs to happen to solve our current problems.

We know we must reel in growth-at-all-costs somehow, and soon, but how do we do it? How can we create a realistic model that goes from our killing the planet and ourselves to a society that works within the boundaries of our limited resources and considers the fragility of our environment? How can we make the necessary changes on a large enough scale, while still providing for millions of people? How can we take the carbon out of our atmosphere and put it back in our soil and begin to reverse the disastrous impacts we have had on our one and only home? What changes can you and I make in our lives, our communities, our habits, our work, and our values to bring about a more just and sustainable world?

THE SOLUTION IS A "MONEYLESS" SOCIETY

The visionary solution to our existential problems is to create a "moneyless" society, but this is a long-term, multigenerational effort—it may even seem undoable. And what does "moneyless" even mean? That's part of what we'll explore in this book.

Let me say that the changes we can make to get to a moneyless society are both large and small, ranging from how we get our food to how we do our work, from how our communities operate to how we travel. Forward-thinking developers are building ecologically friendly, state-of-the-art solutions that place value on working with other people and regenerating our natural resources. Equal-ownership cooperative business models aim to eliminate inequality, increase collaboration and democracy in the workplace, and provide additional layers of job security in times of contraction. Conservation, the sharing economy, and circular economics are becoming the overwhelmingly evident prescriptions for a population that has become disconnected from its source and addicted to consumption. Living, working, and deriving goods locally is a growing trend that is reducing the need to rely on transportation for ourselves and our necessities, while also providing more opportunity for building community resilience and developing new relationships.

These and many other innovations have the potential to dramatically increase the standard of living for nearly everyone on the planet while at the same time reversing much of the damage we have done. The technologies and systems are already here. All that is left is to implement them wisely and let our new approaches revolutionize the ways we work, live, and interact, while simultaneously healing our world.

It is important to note that the needed solutions do not stop at the monetary system. The eventual obsolescence and elimination of the monetary system is a foundational change that has the potential to work harmoniously with many other systemic overhauls, if undertaken carefully and wisely. Healing our planet and achieving long-term sustainability necessitate respecting each other and every facet of our environment and developing a mindset that regards everything as part of Earth's life-supporting ecology.

WHAT IF WE DON'T CHANGE?

What happens if we don't change the foundational structure of our society? Well, maybe not much—to our generation, at least . . . although there is still a strong chance that we are heading off a cliff as far as economic and societal collapse is concerned. Even if our society manages to avoid collapse in the coming decades, our children and our children's children will never forgive us for what we have done to their lives, to their futures, and to their hopes and dreams.

It will be our children and our grandchildren and their children as well who will be displaced by hurricanes and floods; who won't have enough food or clean water; who will succumb to disease, starvation, heat exhaustion, pneumonia, frostbite, respiratory failure from chronic smoke inhalation, and renal failure from dehydration; who will be worn down in mass climate-change-refugee migrations, swept away in floods, crushed in landslides, burned in fires, trampled by rioting masses in civil unrest, or killed by some totalitarian state trying to cling to its last vestiges of power.

If this sounds like a pessimistic view of the future, you are correct. It is pessimistic. It assumes we do nothing, that we stay on our current trajectory. It assumes we let the beast of a society we have unleashed continue to destroy the world around us. We have quite a large train to stop, and not much track left to do it.

There are many who fear it is already too late, that we are beyond the point of no return, across the Rubicon, that we have triggered feedback loops that are now unstoppable and will relentlessly pummel our species into oblivion. I certainly hope that is not the case. More than likely, though, we have years and not decades to make massive changes. The signs are all around us if we are wise enough to see them. We must act decidedly, fast, and *now* should we have any hope of implementing the necessary changes in time.

HOW I CAME TO THIS UNDERSTANDING

When I was fifteen, my mother drove to the top of a nine-story freeway overpass on the northwest side of Houston, got out, and threw herself over the edge of the cement guardrail. When she died, any semblance of certainty in my life came crashing down. I ran away from home and from as many of my problems as I could. I bounced from state to state and worked more jobs than I can count, in search of something that could help me put my life back together.

I loathed the medical system. My mother had been rear-ended in a minor traffic accident, and a routine case of whiplash turned into a nightmare—pain, painkillers, more pain, cervical-fusion surgery, lots more pain, addiction to painkillers, psychosis, and eventually suicide. I blamed the doctors, hospitals, and pharmaceutical companies for her death. Not only that, but I hated the way the world worked—how jobs and employment were so cold, meaningless, and wasteful; how the medical system placed profits before people; how housing was so expensive and that people were allowed to be homeless; how we fought wars over resources, and on and on.

But my real problem was that I had no idea what to do about it.

My father said I should focus on making as much money as possible and that once I was wealthy everything else would fall into place. That idea never seemed to work out though. The polar-opposite idea of going off-grid or living a nomadic exist-ence was alluring, but being a rebellious, promiscuous teenager with few boundaries, soon my girlfriend had given birth to our daughter, and I very much wanted to be part of their lives.

I felt lost and simultaneously stuck in a place I wanted nothing to do with.

Then I came across Peter Joseph's documentary *Zeitgeist: Addendum*,[6] which clearly and concisely laid out the flaws of the monetary system, and presented the designs proposed by The Venus Project as a potential solution. To me, it opened a whole new world of possibilities. Suddenly, the solutions I had been searching for were right in front of me.

What I couldn't understand, however, was why more was not being done to develop the revolutionary systems and constructs described in the movie. Were there no communities of people working together to make this happen? What progress had been made toward these ideals? What were the most effective things we could do to start moving in this direction?

Thus began a journey of discovery. In looking for answers to my questions, I gained a deeper understanding of why the monetary system causes the problems it does. I found many more questions—some without answers—and I found many individuals and organizations working to change the world before it is too late.

In 2013, I created the website MoneylessSociety.com to catalog my findings and share them with others while continuing my explorations. Shortly thereafter, I created the Moneyless Society Facebook page. In late 2020, because we were beginning to receive a good number of visitor posts on our main Facebook page, I created the Facebook group by the same name so that others could post about and discuss the topic. This Facebook group now hosts roughly 25,000 members and has been an invaluable source for new information, networking, and finding like-minded individuals to collaborate with. In 2020, Amanda Smith was the first person to come on board full-time and help with the organization, and in 2021, Amanda and I established Moneyless Society as a nonprofit. Soon after, we created the Moneyless Society podcast (now in its second season of production) with visionary filmmaker Zachary Marlow.

I began writing this book in 2017 as I kept learning and connecting with people. Five years later, it is finally reaching completion.

WHAT TO EXPECT FROM THIS BOOK

In this book I want to share with you what I (and many others) have learned, because you too may be feeling frustration with our current society without being able to articulate exactly *why*.

In Part One of this book, we'll examine many of the ways that capitalism and the monetary system are producing feedback loops and consequences that undermine our ability to live in peace and prosperity and that curtail our planet's ability to sustain life as we know it.

In Part Two, we'll look at new systems and structures that can replace our outmoded monetary system and lead to different results, as well as the transition process and steps people are already taking.

The monetary system is so embedded in society that eliminating it is rarely even acknowledged as a possibility. I make no claim of having all the answers to our problems—many specific solutions will emerge over time, and the evolution to a new form of society will take generations at minimum—but I can help you understand how we got where we are, the path unfolding before us, and the steps you can begin to take to help save our children's future and life as we know it on this planet.

I believe that working together in communities, becoming reoriented with our natural environment, and focusing on creating abundance using sustainable forms of technology is the most effective way we can restore balance to both our lives and the ecosystem around us. If you are looking for actionable, realistic things to do to work toward these types of goals—in your office, your backyard, with your friends, neighbors, and family—then I hope this book can be a helpful resource.

PART ONE

THE PROBLEM

We shall not cease from exploration
And the end of all our exploring
Will be to arrive where we started
And know the place for the first time.

T. S. ELIOT, FROM "FOUR QUARTETS 4: LITTLE GIDDING"

CHAPTER 1

A BRIEF HISTORY OF MONEY & CAPITALISM

No one wants to die. Even people who want to go to heaven don't
want to die to get there. And yet death is the destination we all
share. No one has ever escaped it. And that is as it should be,
because Death is very likely the single best invention of Life. It is
Life's change agent. It clears out the old to make way for the new.

STEVE JOBS

As the good Mr. Jobs noted, death is our common denominator, allowing new life to build upon the achievements of previous generations. Similarly, innovation drives older, less-efficient products and practices into obsolescence. Remember the milkman? The elevator operator? How about the medieval knight? Most of us have heard of these but have never seen any in real life. Technology and modern social arrangements did away with them long ago. Now, milk is easily found at your local grocery store, elevators operate at the push of a button, and, fortunately, most of us no longer need a literal knight in shining armor to protect us from roaming hordes of barbarians. The old systems and structures have been done away with, but at the time of their existence, it would have been hard to imagine what the world would be like beyond what was already established.

Today, myriad systems work together to form the fabric of our economy, society, and daily lives. The world's nations and governments are systems that operate to meet specific needs and fulfill certain purposes. Law is a system. Transportation is a system. Agriculture is a system. We have systems for everything: entertainment, finance, communication, manufacturing, production, education—and even money.

Thanks to technological advancements, the systems that govern our world continue to evolve in scope and complexity, and inevitably, because of this evolution, many of society's needs and logistics will continue to change. For instance, in our modern economy, because businesses are forced to minimize labor costs to stay competitive, it is likely that many of the roles and jobs we are familiar with will be taken by computer programs and robots within the coming decades.

Furthermore, capitalism itself is a system that will likely be phased out in the coming years, along with many of the rules, institutions, and functions its structure entails. The overarching structures of capitalism have grown and developed to such an extent that they have pushed our planet to the limits of its carrying capacity. Because of the increasingly pressing climate crisis—a major symptom of resource overshoot, which we will discuss later—if we are to avoid global catastrophe, we have a relatively short amount of time to overhaul many systems and structures that took hundreds or thousands of years to develop. This is not because capitalism has "failed" per se, but rather because it has provided us with technology that has built a world ripe for the next phase of our socioeconomic evolution. Thus, massive changes seem inevitable. But what do we change? Where do we start? And why is money part of the problem?

To make informed decisions we must first examine the current systems and their results. Once we understand how the various elements of our economy and society have evolved and presently interact with each other, we can look at the feedback loops these relationships produce, and their effects upon our environment and society.

When we talk about money, we are also talking about systems, institutions, practices, and beliefs that have developed (intentionally or inadvertently) in accord with the monetary system and that continue to help it grow in perpetuity—things like debt, trade, corporations, private property, and wage labor. To help us understand what can be done about these issues, let us first take a brief look at some basic systems, how they evolved, and how they have contributed to today's social, economic, and financial dynamics.

LABOR & VALUE

If the Bible had dealt with economics instead of religion, the opening sentence would have read, "In the beginning, people worked." Before there were markets, corporations, cars, factories, houses, money, or anything remotely resembling modern civilization, there was work to be done. Our primitive ancestors labored to make weapons to hunt with, clothing to keep warm, and shelter for safety. According to archeologists, the earliest stone tools, found at Lake Turkana in Kenya, date back 3.3 million years—predating even the earliest humans in the *Homo* genus.[7]

The world we know today was created through labor. It takes labor to cut down trees and turn them into things we can use, such as tables, chairs, and houses. It takes labor to extract oil and metals from the earth and make smartphones, cars, and toaster ovens. Everything we could ever use, need, or want, and that is not already found in nature, was and is created because of human labor.

Since labor can create physical things around us that we use and that benefit us and others, we could say our labor can create *value*. This is not to say we value only what labor has created—we also find value in things such as a beautiful sunset or spending time with loved ones; nor is this to say that all labor creates something valuable. But one of the reasons we value items for sale in our market society is because they require labor to produce.

A worker's labor can contribute value to society long after it's done. Both the washing machine and the dishwasher were first invented in the mid-1800s, but it took nearly a hundred years before they could be made accessible to the average household. Even though the original inventors and workers who built and improved these machines died long ago, the value their labor created will continue to benefit us for generations to come. Similar stories could be told about the telephone, the television, the automobile, and many more of today's common goods and appliances. Our ancestors' contributions can be seen throughout our modern world, in everything from our medical system to our water and sewage infrastructure, the electric grid, the internet, our vehicles and transportation systems, agriculture, governments, and much more.

The value of labor constantly accumulates in the present, allowing us to build upon previous generations' accomplishments. This enables future generations to progress beyond what those before could achieve in their lifetimes.

TRADE, DEBT & MONEY

As soon as our prehistoric ancestors began to make pottery, weapons, and tools, it is likely that they also began to trade them. Archeologists have discovered evidence that suggests the practice of trade may have existed for up to 300,000 years,[8] dating back to the Middle Stone Age in Africa when hunter-gatherer tribes traded tools and weapons with each other.

As the current (Holocene) interglacial period began and the planet warmed, humans flourished and began to exhaust their natural food supply in some areas. This lack of food drove our early ancestors to begin experimenting with various edible plant species, which gradually gave birth to agriculture. The period of transition from a hunter-gatherer lifestyle to agrarian settlements, which began approximately twelve thousand years ago, is known as the Neolithic Revolution. (Note: The most recent anthropological research, as discussed extensively in David Graeber and David Wengrow's *The Dawn of Everything: A New History of Humanity*, points to the existence of many large, complex societies in existence for tens of thousands of years *before* this period. While we know very little about most of these societies, the evidence pointing to a variety of intricate social arrangements only reinforces our knowledge that humans can successfully organize in practically whatever way they seem inclined to choose.)

Through human ingenuity, farmers learned how to produce increasingly larger amounts of grains. Eventually, improvements in agricultural technology, such as irrigation channels, the plow, and the domestication of animals, enabled humans to create a surplus. *Surplus*, in this context, is what is left over from a harvest after storing enough food for one's family and enough seeds for the next crop. Creating an abundance of food as a hunter-gatherer was likely challenging, since most edible wild plants or animals were difficult to obtain and preserve in large quantities, so the ability to create a surplus marked a significant inflection point in human history.

Possessing a surplus of food set the stage for society to grow in scope and complexity, which led to the further specialization of labor. Fewer individuals were needed to focus on food production and therefore could attend to other duties, often concentrating on a specific craft or skill. Specialization of labor gave way to multiple new roles within emerging societies and enabled the formation of large-scale civilizations, such as Sumer in southern Mesopotamia.

The creation of a surplus of grains also created a need for grain storehouses, known as granaries. In ancient Mesopotamia, when farmers deposited their grain, they received small clay tokens that could be returned for the grain in the future. While these early forms of currency were not frequently traded, they served as a basis for the formation of many modern currencies, accounting practices, the tracking and payment of debts, and even written language. In fact, we can trace most Western alphabets directly to the original markings on these ancient tokens.[9]

The functions that currency provided were integral to the development of early civilization. Money stimulated the economy by facilitating the exchange of goods. It allowed people to store wealth beyond what would be reasonable with physical resources such as land, food, or cattle. Money also provided a uniform measurement for exchange, which helped people determine the values of various items and stabilize the prices of goods.

As more currencies were accepted and standardized around the world, money began to take on a value all its own, gradually shifting from being a tool to help people meet their needs and goals to being the need and goal itself.

PROFIT

Profit is any excess money or wealth that a company, person, or institution procures through the course of business and is left after all expenses are paid. You could say that profit is the financial version of surplus. While profit and accumulation of wealth are possible in the absence of money, the introduction of a universal accounting system placed a number value on profit. Being able to quantify profit also created a *focus* on profit, and further incentivized the obtainment of such.

The incentive for profit arises from humans' (as well as most species') susceptibility to a type of operant conditioning called *positive reinforcement*. The principle of positive reinforcement simply means that people are more likely to continue doing things for which they are rewarded. Since we are rewarded for our economic growth and activity with the means for even more economic growth and activity (that is, money), the cycle continues to reinforce itself, increasing in strength, scope, and complexity with each pass.

Profit and the incentive to pursue it are unavoidable mechanisms of the monetary system. The positive reinforcement received when obtaining profits creates a feedback loop that has made the need for profit central to the functioning of our economy. Relatively few goods and services in our society are produced or managed outside the for-profit business model. The result is a society centered around the obtainment of additional surplus wealth, conditioned to endlessly pursue growth, competition, and consumption, and forced to labor for wages to procure everyday necessities.

ARTIFICIAL SCARCITY & CHAOTIC PRODUCTION

In technical terms, *artificial scarcity* is "when individuals are excluded from accessing sufficient resources in a given system" or "when scarcity is induced into a system, when it potentially could have sufficiency or abundance."[10] In practical terms, artificial scarcity is when things are purposefully withheld or restricted from use so they can be sold for profit.

The incentive for profit inherent within the current monetary system ensures the creation of unnecessary, human-imposed limits and restrictions on the accessibility and use of many goods, services, resources, information, permissions, and opportunities. The rules and regulations that reinforce this embedded structure of scarcity create vast amounts of redundant work, a lack of collaboration among organizations, and an overall insufficiency of resources that could otherwise be made abundantly available through sharing or open-access arrangements. The practice of artificial scarcity stands in direct opposition to optimizing sustainable output in concert with public benefit.

Artificial scarcity continues to be sought after and implemented through a variety of mechanisms, many of which are so commonplace in our society that we may not even recognize them as such. Zoning ordinances, for instance, frequently prevent properties from productive uses, often for no purpose other than maximizing property values. Paywalls on websites prevent readers from accessing information that could otherwise be freely shared with virtually no additional cost. Copyrights and patents discourage or prevent companies from freely using or improving upon another's ideas, research, or designs. Planned obsolescence—when products are designed to be less compatible with current technology as time goes on—is often used to coerce consumers to purchase the latest version of something. Many companies have been known to hoard products intentionally or to purposefully delay, restrict, or prevent the release of new technology. Some companies even deliberately destroy their merchandise if it cannot be sold, because storing it costs money and giving it away could lower the price that it might command in the future.

Additionally, while artificial scarcity is intentional (and could be eliminated if we chose to do so), we also find *unintentional* scarcity as a byproduct of the uncoordinated nature of our production and distribution systems. Scarcity is a symptom of the disconnect between producers and why items are produced (for profit) and consumers and why items are used (for practical purposes).

To accurately meet consumer demand without overproducing, producers need to know who needs what, when they need it, where they need it, and so on. In our current economy, there are not enough information systems available to producers to enable them to plan the details of production at that level. Rather they must guess using the limited information they have, which results in producers being inaccurate in their estimates, producing too many or too few of various items, and sometimes being way off in estimating demand. These inaccuracies can create shortages as well as massive price fluctuations—each of which can serve as a catalyst for a full-blown economic crisis.

INDUSTRIALIZATION & THE BIRTH OF CAPITALISM

Capitalism—defined as "an economic and political system in which property, business, and industry are controlled by private owners rather than by the state, with the purpose of making profit"[11]—began to emerge in England in the 1800s, following a series of events that began centuries earlier and that provided the circumstances essential for its formation. Exactly how the transition from feudalism to capitalism took place is still a widely debated topic; however, new technologies likely played a pivotal role in the shift. Key innovations included the compass, the wind-powered sawmill, and improvements in shipbuilding.

As longer shipping routes became more commonly traveled, traders and merchants began to leverage the difference in the value of various goods across Europe and Asia. While goods (such as spices, wine, and wool) rather than money were often used, traders used the same basic idea as our modern investing philosophy: buy low and sell high. Sailors would make multiple stops along their routes, amassing more and more value as they conducted a series of trades to maximize their returns. In this manner, many merchants and traders started to acquire large fortunes.

Lords and nobles in England saw the traders amassing wealth that could soon surpass their own and wanted more wealth for themselves to uphold their status. Since much of the arable land at the time was being farmed by peasants to grow vegetables for eating (which would quickly spoil on long journeys), the lords did not have any significant products to trade. However, one thing they did have that could be traded globally was wool. Unlike vegetables, wool could survive long voyages and was in demand in many areas throughout Europe, Asia, and Africa.

So, during a period known as the *enclosures* (and often under newly passed laws called the Enclosure Acts, which took place roughly 1600–1900), thousands of peasants were forced off their commonly held land to create pastures for raising sheep.

Fences were erected to keep sheep in and people out. Some of the peasants were able to stay and tend to the sheep under various arrangements, but countless individuals and families suddenly found themselves homeless. With no land or means of subsistence, wandering peasants had no choice but to roam the countryside in search of food and shelter in exchange for the only thing they could offer: their labor. This, essentially, was the beginning of the "labor market" as we know it today.

Over time, as many other countries and areas of the world followed England's lead in passing legislation that permitted enclosures, people started erecting fences and enclosing land for many purposes—so much so that the practice of enclosing one's land with a fence is now a common characteristic of modern society. Arguably, as violent and contemptible as the practice of enclosure may have been in its beginning, according to many historians, enclosing land did have some positive effects. Many claim that it prompted people to develop more modern agricultural methods and created greater surplus of both food and labor.

Technology and innovation also continued to play their parts well into the development of capitalism and an industrialized economy. The steam engine, waterpower, iron production, and chemical manufacturing all prompted the creation of even more machines and structures that could mass-produce goods in the pursuit of profits. This was especially true in the textile industry, with the cotton gin and the power loom being two of the most significant machines of early industrialization. Eventually, with the combination of masses of hungry workers, the machinery to produce goods, and enclosed land at property owners' disposal, factories began to spring up filled with newly built machines designed for mass production and an abundance of desperate workers to operate them.

EXPLOITATION

As mentioned earlier, human labor can create things we use and value. In this new arrangement, the land and factory owners were able to negotiate for their workers' labor at relatively low costs, since the workers had no choice but to submit to employment or go hungry and homeless. This arrangement essentially gave the owners the opportunity to keep a portion of the value produced by their workers—in other words, the owners kept the *surplus value*. While giving a lord or noble a portion of the fruits of one's labor was not uncommon under feudal arrangements, factory owners were now able to "capitalize" on both the workers' labor and the machines' production capacity. This enabled the factory owners to create and produce much *more* value.

The everyday operation of capitalism and the market economy in its current state can only be accomplished through *exploitation*, defined as "the use or development of something for profit or progress in business."[12] While most workers can, technically, choose when, where, and to whom they sell their labor, they have no realistic choice but to submit to labor of some sort eventually, since they have no other means of survival. At its core, the relationship between employers and employees is an exploitative relationship, wherein the capitalist, who has the means to purchase land and machines, benefits from the workers' situation by not equitably sharing the full value of the labor or its products with the workers. It is a difficult concept for a lot of people to wrap their heads around, but capitalism, in the most basic sense, is an arrangement centered around exploitation—exploitation of natural resources, of humans, of the environment, of animals, machines, land, air, water, and even of money itself.

In these terms, we are using the word exploitation in both the "neutral" sense of using a resource for your own or someone else's benefit, as well as in the "selfish" sense of a person or entity using someone's labor without giving them an equitable share of the profits. This "selfish" definition of exploitation also applies to situations wherein the workers' compensation may seem satisfactory to the workers, but in which the business owner still receives many times more than the average worker. Many (if not all) of the richest people in the world are prime examples of these exploitative relationships wherein surplus labor value is not equitably shared but rather enriches a few people or even just a single individual at the head of the organization.

COMMODIFICATION

A side effect of money and capitalism is what we could call *commodification*. A *commodity* is anything that is created for sale on the open market or is regularly bought and sold—which now includes practically everything we could ever need or use—so commodification simply means turning something into a "product."

Before capitalism took hold, most families and communities produced goods and items for themselves. Whatever surplus was created could be traded with neighbors or sold in local markets. Nowadays, however, almost *nothing* is produced within a typical household or residential community, and practically everything that an individual or family needs or wants is purchased through markets as a commodity. Furthermore, most necessities have been commodified and can often be difficult or impossible to procure without the money to purchase them.

One of the main catalysts for this development is that three things became commodities that were not treated as such before: land, labor, and the means of production (factories, machines, and so on). These three things are now commonly bought and sold in modern society, and this practice helped form the basis of our current socioeconomic system, capitalism. Without the ability to buy or sell land, labor, or the means of production, capitalism essentially would not exist. It is because these three things became commodities that everything else also became a commodity. We will discuss more of how this happened in a moment.

PRIVATE PROPERTY

One of the foundational pillars of the capitalist system is the concept of private property. The idea of "owning" any sort of property naturally came about because of the investment of labor into land or other tangible resources. If someone put their time and energy into planting a field of wheat, for instance, they would likely also want to protect that investment of labor and, therefore, the fruits of that labor as their own. The same applies to tools, homes, clothing, and many other items that require labor to produce. This is understandable, since most people don't want to lose something that they have worked hard to make. Therefore, the idea of owning property, and its eventual enforcement by law, is a natural evolution of labor and value.

However, things get a bit more complicated when you throw in money. With the use of money, the expenditure of our labor is not required to own or produce things. Because of the Enclosure Acts that put an end to most of the commons, the idea of private property became much more than simply what someone could produce from their own labor. The law of "ownership" now extends to include anything that can be purchased with money, or even with debt, including land, farms, machines, factories, ideas, designs, and more.

Regarding this subject, let's make a couple of quick distinctions about the context in which we use the term "property."

Most people are familiar with the common distinction between public and private property. *Public property* is owned or administered by the government, and *private property* is owned by nongovernmental entities such as individuals or corporations.

Many people are also likely familiar with the distinction between personal property and real property, as in the real estate context. Generally, anything moveable (such as clothes, furniture, vehicles) is referred to as *personal property*, and anything immovable (such as land, homes, buildings, factories) is referred to as *real property*.

We would also like to add a distinction that many people might not be familiar with, however: private property vs. personal property. In the context we're considering, the distinction is as follows:

Personal property includes things that we own and use personally for our own benefit or consumption. Our toothbrushes, our clothing, our furniture, the homes we live in—these can all be considered our personal property because we use them for our own benefit and consumption.

Private property includes businesses, buildings, land, or machinery that is owned or operated for the purpose of making a profit. A rental home, a restaurant, a commercial farm, and large-scale production machinery can all be considered private property since they are owned and operated for the purpose of making a profit.

Note that this distinction differs from the more common context of private versus public (that is, government-owned) property. Private property, in the context of this book, is the rule of law that dictates that a single person or entity (such as a corporation) can exclusively own, control, and profit from factories, resources, farmland, and machines of mass production. The Enclosure Acts that kicked people off the common land so it could be used instead to generate profits were essentially the beginning of the private property laws that we know today. The legal system also says that property owners can keep whatever amount of their laborers' value they are able to negotiate. Because of these mechanisms, the law of private property is one of the fundamental subsystems of capitalism that perpetuates inequality and exploitation in modern society.

COMPETITION & GROWTH

In capitalism, no company or entity is immune to bankruptcy. Because of the competitive nature of our market economy, the only way corporations can hope to survive in the long run is to grow. If companies do not continuously focus on becoming more competitive, expanding their market share, offering new products, buying other companies, and reducing labor costs, eventually their competitors may put them out of business.

The bigger corporations become, the more aspects of production and distribution they can control. They can streamline more aspects of their business and save more money. They have access to larger amounts of capital for new side ventures. It becomes easier to bankrupt or buy up competitors, break into and dominate markets, and consolidate and centralize control and ownership. Amazon, which had its humble beginnings as an online book retailer, is a prime example (pun intended). In less than thirty years, Amazon has acquired or started more than a hundred different companies, spanning multiple sectors and including film production, autonomous vehicles, pharmaceuticals, shoe sales, cloud storage, a grocery chain, and private space flight.

The fact that companies are forced to adopt this practice of growth and competition creates enough problems in and of itself; however, it is compounded by the fact that it is not just companies that are forced to compete—*everyone* is forced to compete. Just as companies are not immune to bankruptcy, people are not immune to homelessness and starvation. Everyone is competing in some way, often simply for survival, from the ranchers in Brazil slashing away at the rainforest to make more pastureland for grazing, to a mother of three who works in retail and drives for Uber in her spare time. Even laborers on the bottom rung of the ladder are forced to compete with other laborers in the job market in order to pay their rent. We compete for jobs. We compete to get into schools. We compete for clients. We compete for homes and other forms of property.

If we are not wealthy enough to supply our own necessities, we are forced to commoditize our time and labor. And once a person's survival needs are met, they often move on to compete for more resources, property, comfort, security, influence, wealth, power, respect, fame, privilege, notoriety, legacy, and so on. The competition never ends.

All this endless competition and growth keeps perpetuating endless activity, which is a must to keep the capitalist system functioning from one day to the next. This endless activity creates problems, however . . .

MORE MONEY, MORE PROBLEMS

How many times have you heard the phrase "in the good old days"? With all the complexity we experience daily, it's no wonder we long for the past, when life actually was a bit simpler (though in many respects not necessarily better). But, of course, technology keeps racing ahead of us. The financial sector is certainly no exception to the rule, though whether for better or worse is subjective.

As time passes and our society and economy expand and evolve, trade also increases in scope, scale, and complexity. Because nearly everything people need to survive is now commodified and must be acquired through a transaction of some sort, more trade is continually needed to keep our ever-growing population and economic system functioning. In turn, since more trade is needed, more money is also needed to act as a medium of exchange to facilitate the increasing amounts of trade. More complex methods of trade also come into existence, and new technologies and methods of deriving profits surface.

Cowrie shells (small, white, pasta-looking shells) were commonly used as currency for thousands of years in many parts of Africa, Asia, and Europe. Could you imagine paying your rent with shells? Or your cell phone bill? The thought is ridiculous, first because there are nowhere near enough cowrie shells to go around, and second because of the physical difficulty in conducting those transactions. Cowrie shells were phased out, just as paper money is close to being phased out. Compared to digital currency, paper is slow, cumbersome, and inefficient, and it can't travel long distances through a computer instantly, something required more and more these days.

Capitalism's constant, inherent need for more money and growth is why the US had no choice but to finally abandon the last vestiges of the gold standard in 1971 (though the move away from it began with FDR back in 1933). Other countries had begun to suspect that the US did not have enough gold in the Federal Reserve to back the dollar and began to cash in their dollars for gold at the then agreed-upon rate of $35 per ounce. The Nixon administration saw that what amounted to a run on the bank was happening on an international level and that the US dollar was about to lose its credibility if it could not meet the obligations. As a result, Nixon's Treasury Department in 1973 broke the direct convertibility of the dollar to gold, creating our current worldwide floating fiat currency system.

To sustain the ever-growing and increasingly complex methods of trade and commerce, new money must be continually infused into the system. More people need more money for more commodities than ever before. As common as they are today, mortgages became popular only in the 1930s; before then, if you could not buy a home outright, you were usually out of luck. Vehicles are on a long list of things that didn't even exist a couple hundred years ago that many people now make monthly payments on. More innovative methods of conducting transactions are also continuously invented to facilitate trade within the system—financing, payment agreements, and credit card accounts, and, more recently, cryptocurrencies and NFTs (non-fungible tokens).

To compete at scale, companies must often raise larger amounts of capital and utilize newer, more complex financial instruments. Startup costs are now often too high for individuals to fund a new business on their own. Often, entrepreneurs have to sell their ideas to angel investors or venture capitalists, or take on bond debt to raise the required amounts.

Growth and complexity also drive a need for new and creative ways to generate profits. To this end, even money is treated as a commodity; different currencies are bought, sold, and traded worldwide for speculation and profit, and banks gamble with *financial derivatives* (bets or contracts derived from various types of underlying financial assets). The derivatives market, which played a role in the 2008 financial crisis, is larger than ever, often estimated to be more than $1 *quadrillion.*[13]

THE CONSEQUENCES OF THE PRICE MECHANISM

One of the most fundamental problems with capitalism is its tendency to reduce everything to a single interpretation of value: *price*. This is a problem because an item's price gives us little to no information about many other relevant factors, such as working conditions, pollutive effects, or any other detrimental effect.

As we mentioned previously, we often value things because they are useful or do something for us. We call this type of value an item's *use value*, or *utility*. An item's use value is simply what it can be used for and is not determined in numbers. A chair, for instance, has a use value of providing a place to sit.

An item's price can be called its *exchange value*, that is, the value of a commodity when it is traded. Because the capitalist system focuses primarily on exchange value, the main incentive and driver for production lies in creating goods (and situations) that enable business owners to reap the highest prices for their products. But an item's price (exchange value) tells us little except how much money a company is asking for a particular item, or what the market is willing to pay for such an item. It gives us no idea how many people want or can use the item, how many can afford it, what specific use it provides, how much labor it took to produce, the resources that were used in its production, or the environmental impacts of production. When children are forced to mine cobalt in Africa for pennies a day, or local companies outsource their labor to sweatshops in Bangladesh, or a delicate habitat is destroyed to produce a barrel of oil, we cannot rely on an item's price to accurately reflect the human or environmental cost.

One thing we could say is that the price system largely ignores an item's *ecological value*. How many trees did it take to make that stack of paper? What effects will chopping down those trees have? What long-term consequences will those actions and processes have on our environment, our water quality, or our children's future? Ecological value is difficult to quantify in numbers and profits. Something's ecological value includes its relationships and purposes within its greater environment. An arbitrary price cannot capture that complexity. And that is why we need a different, more complex way of thinking, which we will begin to cover in the next chapter.

CRISIS CYCLES: OVEREXPANSION & OVERPRODUCTION

As a society, we are constantly being driven to consume, work, and generate activity. Clever marketing campaigns relentlessly condition and compel us to keep buying and spending. When consumer spending grows, the economic system is relatively stable. When consumer spending is on the decline, however, the economy slows and starts to contract. Jobs are lost, businesses are shuttered, and lenders tighten their standards. Then people start mentioning the most dreaded words in economics: "recession" and "depression."

What makes this happen, however, is often overlooked. The cause is the drive for production, consumption, and growth—inherent to the capitalist system—which produces cycles of expansion and contraction. In the good times (expansion) banks allow their borrowers (whether companies or individuals) to borrow more and more until they overextend themselves, producing or buying more than is needed. Once the system cannot expand at the pace that is needed to sustain the excessive amount of growth, the economy contracts and a crisis occurs. This contraction usually happens because some sort of physical limitation surfaces that prevents part of the system from keeping up with the rate of economic growth. Often the breaking point is when consumer demand cannot absorb an overproduction of goods.

The main problem with this competition- and growth-based system being the default mode of production is that companies are continuously incentivized and motivated to keep expanding and creating new products, regardless of the human or environmental consequences. This never-ending need for new products is evidenced in things like the partial repeal of the 1933 Glass-Steagall Act, which since the Great Depression had prohibited banks from speculating with consumer deposits. Having been chipped away at over the years through legislation and loopholes, the act itself was largely repealed by Congress during the Clinton administration in 1999. This let banks "diversify their product offerings and thus their sources of revenue" and made them "better equipped to compete in global financial markets."[14] Unfortunately, numerous economists now tie that "diversification" to the financial crisis of 2007–2008.

In the early 2000s, to help stimulate the economy after the burst of the dot-com bubble (the previous crisis brought about by overproduction), the Fed and other banks relaxed lending standards and offered low variable rates to borrowers. This increased demand for homes, driving home prices and new home construction to astronomical heights. However, by June 2004 housing prices were skyrocketing and, sensing an overheated market, then-chair of the Federal Reserve Alan Greenspan began raising interest rates; his successor, Ben Bernanke, followed with more increases in 2006. Predictably, many borrowers' monthly payment amounts increased, demand faded, and housing prices declined. By 2007, many people owed more than their homes were worth and could no longer afford their mortgage. Then, disastrously, in 2008 the market was flooded with properties as nearly ten million people lost their homes.

Banks had packaged these personal home loans into "mortgage-backed securities" and sold them to large investment firms, who bought them for their clients. When homeowners went into default and the investments began to fail, several major institutions went bankrupt. As most of us know (and the rest of us learned), many of the large financial institutions are extremely interconnected, and the failure of one can cause a chain reaction that threatens to collapse the rest of the system. The government's response was to bail out the companies with taxpayer money, with little more than a slap on the wrist for the reckless lending practices and overexpansion that created the crisis in the first place.

Yet the system continues to expand at breakneck speed without regard to the brick wall now directly in front of us and plainly in sight. The Federal Reserve cannot raise interest rates to slow the system anymore without causing a miniature stock market crash, because the economy must keep growing at all costs to survive. The biggest financial institutions in the world are all now larger and more interconnected than ever before, [15] and still largely unregulated. What's more, expansion is often seen as a good thing rather than as a symptom of the dysfunction inherent in the system. If anything, we have tried to fix our problems with more of what created them to begin with. As we will learn in the next chapter, the technical term for this is *fixes that fail*.

TWO MAJOR EXTERNALITIES: INEQUALITY & RESOURCE OVERSHOOT

We mentioned earlier that exchange value, or price, does not capture all the true costs of a product or service. *Externalities* are those side effects or consequences that are generally not reflected in the price. They are the "outside" problems that capitalism and its affiliated systems and structures cause.

Most externalities fall into one of two categories: *inequality* or *resource overshoot*. The first of these, inequality, is a direct consequence of the competitive marketplace and *hoarding*—keeping more than one really needs—that occurs under the capitalist system. Inequality and hoarding, and the subsequent wealth gap they create, are seen in instances such as banks foreclosing on people's homes, businesses being bankrupted or bought up by competition, labor being outsourced to other countries, poverty, and cyclical financial crises that transfer massive amounts of wealth from the working class to the wealthiest 1 percent. We will explore more of the causes and effects of inequality in Chapters 3 and 4.

The second of these two categories, resource overshoot, encompasses myriad other problems, and happens when humans (or another species) outgrow or overuse the capacity of their environment in some way. Resource overshoot is occurring because we have been living beyond the means of what our planet can provide, without the proper investments back into the earth, technology, society, or our economy. Most people haven't noticed, because we haven't run out of resources quite yet.

Besides situations wherein we exhaust our supply of a finite resource, resource overshoot also encompasses situations where we are producing too much waste (including greenhouse gases like carbon dioxide, methane, and nitrous oxide) and do not have the capabilities to contain it. Resource overshoot includes effects such as deforestation, overfishing, lithium or cobalt shortages, ocean dead zones, the bleaching of coral reefs, and climate change.

In essence, if our planet were a household, our cupboards

would be nearly empty and our trash cans would be over-flowing. Not only are we running out of resources to harvest (and destroying entire ecosystems in the process), but we are running out of places to put our trash. If we are to have any hope of containing or reversing our destruction, we must seek ways to enable a controlled economic contraction while simultaneously maximizing balance with our natural world.

THE DEATH OF CAPITALISM

Capitalism ultimately exploits and destroys both the earth and everything that depends on it, and it will ensure devastation on a scale beyond anything we can fathom. With the profit motive governing most of the economic activity on the planet today, humans are rapidly making the earth uninhabitable in many places, and the cascading consequences of our actions will result in nothing short of a planetary disaster in the long run. If we care about our children's future, we have no choice but to step back and determine how we can reel in the day-to-day economic activity on which our society depends and replace it with something more sustainable and just.

New and existing technologies, managed with care and with respect to maintaining balance in our environment, can provide all our necessities and more. And that presents us with a choice: do we cling to our old systems and structures, or do we embrace opportunity and create abundance in new, creative ways? We cannot do both.

The properties inherent in the monetary system we have touched upon in this chapter conflict directly with the new paradigms and practices that solving our problems requires. We cannot continue to use a monetary system with an inherent need for growth and at the same time try to implement a system that respects the limits of nature and the dignity of all life. If we want real progress, we must actively choose to leave behind old systems and develop new, sustainable ways to work and live.

CHAPTER 2

SYSTEMS THINKING

No one can define or measure justice, democracy, security,
freedom, truth, or love. No one can define or measure any value.
But if no one speaks up for them, if systems aren't designed to
produce them, if we don't speak about them and point toward
their presence or absence, they will cease to exist.

DONELLA H. MEADOWS, *THINKING IN SYSTEMS: A PRIMER*

N ow that we've looked at the evolution of our monetary system and gained a better understanding of how our current system has been shaped by past circumstances, let's take a short dive into a methodology that can help us grasp the compounding effects of this system: systems thinking. Systems thinking can show us not only how the monetary system has created the effects we are currently witnessing but also the implications for our future. For me, discovering systems thinking was like turning on a light bulb in a room where I was previously fumbling around in the dark. I could feel there were pieces of things that I understood, but I could never look around and see the big picture, or how all the pieces fit together to create a whole. Systems thinking provided that big picture.

Systems thinking, or *systems theory*, is a methodological approach to analysis and problem solving that examines the causes, effects, relationships, and feedback loops between different elements in our world, and how they interact and compound with one another over time to produce various results.

Systems theory also acknowledges that many systems cannot be fully understood. Imagine trying to map out a forest. Could you ever distinguish and list all the complex interactions and relationships between the birds, insects, trees, earth, and weather patterns? No. So we must work with what we do know, while also acknowledging there is much we don't. We must work with an understanding that if we change one aspect of a system, it will affect many other known and unknown elements and can lead to both expected and unexpected outcomes.

Systems thinking helps explain the relationships and feedback mechanisms that govern our society and natural world. The monetary system supports and enables countless other systems that lead to many unfavorable outcomes. Whether it be intentionally or unintentionally, directly or indirectly, overtly or covertly, the systems in place keep many of us locked in a struggle to eke out a better life—and they now even threaten our existence. Once we understand the cause-and-effect relationships between our socioeconomic systems and oppression, violence, racism, sexism, poverty, pollution, resource overshoot, climate change, and more, we realize these things do not happen randomly, but rather by design.

The more we examine our core beliefs, social systems, and the myriad relationships within the systems, the more apparent the causes of our problems become. And once we understand how systems work, rarely do we lose that understanding. Instead, we begin to see connections everywhere in the world around us.

But systems thinking is not all about problems. Systems theory can help us illustrate methods for integrating human society with complex natural systems in a synergistic manner. It can help us solve problems in a more holistic manner.

While this book cannot encompass a full course on systems thinking, which is an extensive field, we will cover a few of the basics to help understand the bigger picture of the monetary system. (If you are interested in exploring systems thinking further, please visit our list of books on the subject at MoneylessSociety.com/books.)

IMPORTANT PRINCIPLES FOR SYSTEMS THINKING

Systems theory outlines a general progression of systems from *simple* to *complicated* and finally to *complex*, with each level growing increasingly more elaborate and unpredictable.

Simple systems are those in which all elements are easily described and understood and there is a well-defined relationship between cause and effect. Eating is a system that satisfies your hunger. A shoe is a system that protects your foot. A pen is a system for writing. Once you know how the system works, the results are predictable and easily duplicated. For this reason, simple systems often resemble processes or procedures, such as playing a song on the piano or baking a cake. I know that if I combine certain ingredients and put them in the oven, something at least partially resembling a cake will come out, and not a hippopotamus or Mick Jagger. Simple systems can also define the relationship between, say, the floor and my pen. If I let go of my pen, gravity will immediately pull it down to the floor. I know that I am not going to get some other result, like the pen powering on my television or flying away.

Complicated systems typically have more elements and more

interrelationships than simple systems. Think of something like an airplane or a large commercial building, or even their individual subsystems, such as a jet engine or electrical system. While you (or more likely an experienced team of people) can diagram a complicated system or execute a complicated process, the nature and scale of the problem being solved, the interconnectedness of all the elements, and the expertise required are what define a complicated system as such. Complicated systems generally require a much greater degree of proficiency and cooperation than simple systems do. This book touches on many complicated systems in fields such as robotics, automation, conservation, transportation, and energy.

Complex systems have numerous interrelated parts and often exhibit behavior that is not predictable even when the parts are (relatively) understood. These types of systems include things like a forest ecosystem, the stock market, or the human brain. Creating desired outcomes within complex systems typically requires much more discussion, reflection, cooperation, openness, honesty, and ability to look at the situation from different perspectives than it does within simple and complicated systems. It's important to recognize that complex systems are dynamic and constantly evolving. Some of the complex systems that are germane to our purposes in this book include the natural environment, politics, economics, the monetary system, war, education, and communities.

Interconnectedness is a fundamental concept in systems thinking. Everything is connected to everything else through myriad systems; nothing exists in a vacuum. In some form or fashion, practically all life on this planet depends on other forms of life for survival; through the systems of society and nature, humans are connected with all the other living things on this planet. Systems thinking offers numerous avenues for analysis of this interconnectedness. Just as a forest is interconnected with all its various parts—trees, insects, birds, sunlight, air, water, bacteria—in ways we will never completely understand, so too are cities and economies interconnected, with relationships affecting parts of numerous subsystems.

Often, in attempting to solve problems, we fail to consider them in light of the interconnectedness and complexity that may have caused or contributed to the problems in the first place. For example, we try to solve the problem of crime by throwing people in jail, but we do nothing to improve the communities the perpetrators came from; we treat symptoms of diseases while doing nothing to improve the environmental or nutritional circumstances that caused them; we try to solve inequality by putting in place a few new laws or regulations without addressing the systemic issues that created the inequality to begin with. Eventually the problems spiral out of control because we have not addressed their root causes. Systems thinking helps us understand and solve these types of problems.

Patterns are situations that repeat themselves in similar fashion throughout nature and society in many ways, and they often are ignored or go unnoticed. Recognizing and labeling patterns helps us predict outcomes in a variety of circumstances. We can see patterns in things like long-term effects on children who are regularly exposed to domestic violence or drug abuse, or crime rates in an area after a major employer outsources its jobs to another country.

In systems thinking these repeating patterns are defined as distinct *archetypes*. In this book, we will cover four archetypes:

Success to the successful means that when you are already successful, it becomes easier to gain more success. For example, if you have achieved financial success in business, then you will find it easier to get a business loan than someone who has not yet achieved financial success. If you have more money, you can invest in providing your children with better education, more technology, and so on, leading to their having more success than someone without such resources. (Sadly, the reverse is true as well. When you have fewer financial resources, you have fewer opportunities, and you pay more for loans, for insurance, and so on.)

Tragedy of the commons occurs when we share a resource but individuals are incented to act in their own interest at the expense of others; as a result, the resource is damaged or depleted, affecting everyone. For example, overfishing is not caused by one fishing boat, but the depletion affects everyone. Putting greenhouse gases in the atmosphere is not one person's fault, but it becomes everyone's problem.

Fixes that fail are solutions that actually exacerbate the original problems. When we attempt to solve a problem by addressing only the symptoms rather than the root cause, we are likely to attempt a fix that fails. For example, if a farmer finds their well is running dry, they may dig a new one; this may solve the problem in the short run. However, if the real problem is the falling water table, then digging a new well only exacerbates the problem. The war on drugs, for example, was intended to reduce drug use but instead caused a booming market for illicit drugs.

Conflicting goals is a pattern that occurs when the pursuit of two goals (which can both be good ones) at odds with one another results in decisions that repeatedly contribute to the success of one goal to the detriment of the other. For instance, many people would like to make more money and also spend more time with their family. Unfortunately, for most individuals, making more money comes at the cost of less time with the family, and vice versa.

We will explore more specific examples of these archetypes in Chapters 3 and 4.

Causality simply means one thing causes another. (However, as our friends in statistics would remind us, correlation is not causation, so be sure to distinguish the two.) In systems thinking, causality is often thought of in cyclical terms and expressed in feedback loops, with an understanding that the systems are dynamic, constantly changing, and evolving entities. A *feedback loop* is the sequence in a cause-and-effect relationship where the output of the process is returned as an input. If you have ever put a live microphone too close to a speaker, you have experienced a feedback loop. The sound coming out of the speaker gets picked up by the microphone and is almost instantly rebroadcast and amplified to a deafeningly loud, high-pitched tone.

Feedback loops are extremely common in our world; all sorts are found in nature, biology, physics, psychology—and even in the economy. When we can recognize different feedback loops in the world around us and pinpoint their causes, it also helps us figure out the most effective ways to change them. Feedback loops, also known as *causal loops*, come in two varieties: reinforcing and balancing.

A *reinforcing feedback loop* occurs when the outcome of a certain action or situation perpetuates conditions that produce more of the same result, creating a self-reinforcing loop of cause and effect. This is also called a *positive feedback loop*, though that does not mean the outcome itself is positive (just as a positive medical test may indicate a negative outcome, such as the presence of an illness). As we briefly mentioned in the first chapter, in psychology positive feedback is also known as *positive reinforcement*—essentially a reward for performing a desired behavior, which encourages more of that same behavior. Usually a reinforcing feedback loop grows with each passing cycle until some outside force balances it out.

A classic example of a reinforcing feedback loop is the human population. Figure 1 shows a *causal loop diagram* for that system. In it you will see two simple elements of the system: *births* and *population*. The arrows from each to the other show that there is a relationship between the two elements. That is, each one affects the other. The plus signs indicate that, all other things being equal, when one level rises, so does the other; when births increase, population increases; as population increases, the number of births increases.

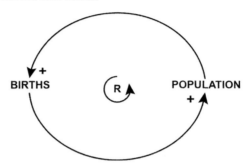

Figure 1: Causal Loop Diagram of Human Population (Births)

The "R" in the circular arrow in the center indicates that this is a *reinforcing loop*. As we have more children and the population grows, we have *more* children, who have the capacity to have even *more* children, and the cycle repeats itself. Often (but not always) reinforcing feedback loops become destructive to a larger system, because once a certain point is reached, the system hits some sort of outside limit and either plateaus or collapses. Probably the most important example of this in the modern world is the reinforcing feedback loops that are happening with greenhouse gas release and global warming. As greenhouse gases are released, the atmosphere warms up; the hotter the atmosphere gets, the more greenhouse gases are released in various ways (more permafrost melting, more forest fires, and so on). We will discuss this topic further in Chapter 4.

A *balancing feedback loop* is one that keeps bringing something back to a certain level or equilibrium. Balancing loops are also called *negative feedback loops*, though again that does not mean the outcome itself is negative. In Figure 2, we've added a second loop to our human population system: to the right of the original loop for *births*, we now have a balancing loop for *deaths*, with *population* as a shared point for the two loops.

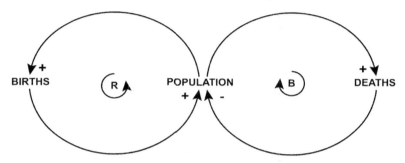

Figure 2: Causal Loop Diagram of Human Population (Births & Deaths)

Note that the "B" in the circular arrow in the center of the loop for deaths indicates it is a balancing loop, and the loop consists of one positive and one negative arrow instead of two positive arrows (as with births and population). Now notice how the two cycles interact: as the population grows, there are more deaths; however, as people die, the population decreases. The balancing loop of deaths prevented humans from undergoing an unsustainable population explosion long ago; without death, an estimated 107 billion people would currently be alive. (Actually, that estimate doesn't consider the number of additional births over a theoretical never-ending lifetime, so the number would be even higher!)

Notice also that the plus and minus signs tell you about the relationship between each set of elements and whether one element affects the other directly or inversely. So, for example, the birth loop says that if births increase, the population increases. This is a direct relationship, which also means that if births decrease, the population decreases. The death loop says that if deaths increase, population decreases. This is an inverse relationship, which also means that if deaths decrease (with all else being equal), population increases.

As you read a systems diagram, the trick is to know what the starting point is—is the item under discussion increasing or decreasing?—and then read the pluses and minuses for each relationship correctly (direct or inverse). It is also important to note that, as in multiplication, two minus signs in a loop cancel each other out and equal a positive. We will see several examples of this in the next chapter.

Additionally, we must pay attention to the relative strengths of reinforcing and balancing loops. While the strength of the birth and death loops is not depicted in this diagram (although more complex models can depict this), in our world the balancing loop (deaths) is currently not as strong as the reinforcing loop (births), and thus the total human population continues to grow.

Other common examples of balancing loops include a thermostat being activated to bring a room back to a specified temperature when it gets too hot or too cold, and predator-prey relationships in the wild that keep populations in check. When one occurrence moves the system toward an unbalanced state, another brings the system back to homeostasis.

Cascade effects, or *cascading effects*, are outcomes or events that occur in a chain, with one occurrence affecting something else, which in turn affects something else, and so on and so forth. One of the classic examples of a cascade effect is when a top predator is eliminated from an ecosystem by activities such as hunting or commercial development. Generally, the elimination of a predator tends to result in the overpopulation of its prey, which in turn causes its own set of problems. A video from Sustainable Human titled *How Wolves Change Rivers* explains what happened when wolves were returned to their natural habitat in Yellowstone National Park eighty years after hunting had virtually eliminated them: The deer population started to avoid the open spaces, especially around the wide-open river valleys and, after decades of overgrazing by the deer, the plants around those areas started to regenerate. The new foliage provided homes and food for numerous species, such as mice, hawks, and bears, which returned to the area. The better plant and root structures also improved the integrity of the riverbanks and held them in place, which meant less riverbank lost to erosion and rivers that tended to meander less.

The nature of cascade effects can be subtle, and often surprising. Second-, third-, and fourth-order consequences can occur and compound with each other in so many ways that illustrating all of their possible relationships and repercussions can be a monumental, if not impossible, task. But for instance, one of the cascade effects of the processed food that is eaten by many Americans might look something like this: Unhealthy food is consumed by a large percentage of the population. This, in turn, contributes to deteriorating health of the population overall, which puts a greater demand on the medical system, driving up prices for healthcare, salaries for doctors, and the number of available positions. Since healthcare pays better than many other fields, more students turn to the healthcare industry as a career path instead of, say, engineering or IT. This, in turn, decreases the pace of technological innovations in those other fields. And the chain of effects goes on.

In complex systems, we often see *counterintuitive* results, meaning we expect one outcome and something else happens. For example, we might think that increasing the amount of fertilizer on a crop would improve the yield. And indeed, if we increase the amount of fertilizer by a small amount, we may get an increase in crop yield. However, if we increase the fertilizer dramatically, the crops will die, because the quantity of fertilizer has become toxic, and we'll get nothing. Our earlier example of the drug war also generated counterintuitive results; one might have expected that making drugs illegal and putting dealers in jail would deter and reduce drug use, but doing so has actually increased consumption.

In many systems we find *stocks* and *flows*, two common, interrelated principles. *Stock* is how much of something there is in some definable measure, or how much has built up over time. When you have a supply of something, you are said to have a stock of it—a stock of potatoes, corn, computers, trees, water, oil, or even human population. *Flow* is the rate at which that stock builds or depletes.

A common analogy to understand stock and flow is a bathtub. Whatever water is in the tub is its stock, and the rate at which the tub is filling and/or draining is the flow. A key thing to remember is that the tub can be filling and draining at the same time. (In the human population system, people are dying and being born at the same time.) Often, the idea with stock and flow is to synchronize the rate of input and output in the "tub" so that the flow is constantly moving but the level of stock remains the same. This concept can also apply to replenishing a stock with something new/improved at the same rate that old/outdated stock is being used or discarded.

Stocks and flows are found in many systems; however, for the sake of simplicity, we have left them out of our diagrams. The main point is to understand that in systems thinking, stocks are the things you can count or measure, and the flow is the rate at which they move around, and that both measurements affect the dynamics of how a system operates and interacts with other systems or the rest of the world.

Analysis is the taking apart of something to understand the pieces. *Synthesis*, on the other hand, is the combination of multiple elements to create something new. It is also the act of understanding the whole and recognizing how individual elements relate to and interact with one another. Synthesis occurs in many ways all around us—in living organisms, mechanical objects, institutions. If you were to disassemble all thirty thousand or so parts of your car and lay them out on the ground, aside from creating a ton of work for yourself, you could analyze the pieces, but you would have taken away the synthesis of those parts working together to form a car. When you put them all back together in the correct manner, you form an object that functions in a way that was impossible when the pieces were separate. Synthesis also occurs within organizations that are aligned toward a specific cause or purpose, such as all the branches of government working together to form a wholly operating system, or a computer manufacturer that utilizes multiple other manufacturers and suppliers to produce a desired laptop.

Emergence is the outcome of synergy; it is the process of things coming together in a self-organizing way and forming something new that takes on properties not found in any of its constituent parts. Emergence is the sand dunes that are carved out by patterns of wind and aerodynamics. It is a hurricane forming out of water vapor and fluctuations in temperature. It is a caterpillar morphing into a butterfly. Emergence is all around us in the universe, and we also have an opportunity to participate in creating something new out of the circumstances before us. The new, sustainable systems that can potentially emerge from our current plight are the focus of this book.

LEVERAGE POINTS IN SYSTEMS

When we understand a complex system (to the extent possible), we can begin to understand the root causes of problems and begin to look for ways to change the system to solve those problems. *Leverage points* are the specific places we can make a change in the system that will influence the outcome. Think of the base word "lever" and your high school physics class: when you use a lever, you can lift a weight that you would not be able to lift on your own, and the longer the lever, the greater the weight you can lift. One of the main objectives of systems theory is to identify the changes that make the greatest impact with the least amount of effort or resistance; in other words, we want the "long" levers. (Unfortunately, because levers are often counterintuitive, we sometimes push them the wrong direction, so things get systemically worse rather than better.)

The late Donella Meadows, one of the best-known authors and researchers on systems theory, proposed the following twelve classifications of leverage points to intervene in a system, in order from least effective to most effective.[16]

12. Constants, parameters, numbers. These are numbers that can be changed, but the system itself functions the same way. For example, you can change the corporate tax rate or soybean subsidy amount, but the system itself works the same way.

11. The size of buffers and other stabilizing stocks, relative to their flows. Think about the difference between a leak in a bucket and the same size leak in a huge reservoir; the impact on the bucket is much bigger because the stock is so much smaller. In a business context, compare a month's inventory supply versus a three-day supply; a disruption in the supply chain will impact the three-day setup much more than the one that holds a greater inventory.

10. Structure of material stocks and flows. A good example of the structure of stocks and flows is your plumbing system. How does the water flow if the pipes are straight versus if they are bent numerous times? Another example is the road system—I am sure you can think of problematic intersections where you get stuck regularly (and you probably know exactly how to redesign them). When something is built poorly, one solution is to rebuild, but it is almost always better to invest in a good design up front, also known as *intentional design* or *purposeful design*. Some structures, of course, are built into nature, and we do not get to change them—for example, the aging process of the population. We cannot change how long it takes for someone to grow up; it takes a certain number of years to reach physical maturity.

9. Length of delays relative to the rate of system changes. When you make a change in a system, how quickly do you see a new result? That is, what's the delay time? A common example to explain the impact of delays is the hot water tap. The closer the water heater is to the faucet, the faster the hot water comes out when you turn the tap. If the water heater is in the basement and must travel to the second floor, there is a longer delay in getting hot water than there would be if the water heater were in the next room. Another example: when there is high housing demand, developers build more houses, but building takes time; by the time the houses are finished, the demand may have changed.

8. Strength of negative feedback loops relative to the effect they are trying to correct against. As mentioned in the population example, positive and negative feedback loops can have different strengths; in most countries the birth rate is higher than the death rate, so we have growing populations. As countries become wealthier and have access to things like education and birth control, we typically see a reduction in the birth rate, weakening that reinforcing cycle and potentially leading to a declining population if the rate goes low enough.

7. The gain around positive feedback loops. Positive feedback loops are reinforcing. The rate at which they grow—their momentum, or gain—affects the system and how soon it will collapse if there is not a balancing loop. For instance, at some of the beaches in San Diego, signs state that feeding the squirrels is illegal. When people bring bread and other food for the squirrels, that increases the gain of the positive feedback loop of squirrel births, causing the population to explode. Then after tourist season, the food runs out. What the "do not feed the squirrels" signs do not tell you is the grim result: at some point the squirrel overpopulation must be dealt with (by poison or other means) to prevent them from eating each other.

6. Structure of information flow. Who has (and does not have) access to what kinds of information and feedback? When you see feedback regularly, you are more likely to use it. In one classic example, half the houses in a subdivision had their electricity meter in the front hall and half had it in the basement. The residents of the houses with meters in the front hall had lower electric bills simply because they knew how much they were using. If information is missing or difficult to find, it can cause the system to move toward an unbalanced state.

5. Rules of the system. Rules include things like incentives, punishments, and constraints. When driving, red means stop; green means go. Contracts lay out the rules of a business engagement. Rules range from strong, such as the law of gravity, to weak, such as social agreements like "don't cut in line."

4. Power to add, change, evolve, or self-organize system structure. The ability to "self-organize" means the ability to change any or multiple other leverage points that have come before this—changing rules, adding feedback loops, changing the structure of stocks or flows. In biology, species evolve. In a company, workers may form a union, or teams may have the authority to structure their project work the way they want. Machine learning is a technological advancement that continuously changes how the system works.

3. Goal or purpose of the system. Purposefulness is one of the most crucial determinants of how systems operate and their eventual outcomes and consequences. You can take an organization or a system with certain factors and relationships, and when you give it a different purpose, the outcomes and consequences change. For example, you could have a kitchen that roasts Thanksgiving turkeys all day long, but your purpose—say, making a profit versus feeding homeless people—makes all the difference. In one instance, your turkeys end up on a shelf at Walmart, and in the other, they end up on a table at a homeless shelter.

2. Mindset or paradigm from which the system arises. Where do the goals, structures, rules, delays, and parameters come from? What mindset, beliefs, or assumptions are they founded on? The importance of growth and profit are assumptions that are foundational to the structure of our society, which is predominantly built around the monetary system. What if the mindset shifted from a competition-based paradigm like "How can I get everything I need?" to a collaboration-based paradigm like "How can we work together so we all get everything we need?" Changing paradigms can be both easy and difficult. It does not cost anything to change your mindset, but it does entail giving up the prior paradigm. One example of a recent broad paradigm shift occurred following the murder of George Floyd; a significant portion of the US population shifted from thinking racism was a relatively limited problem to understanding how fully it is embedded in our present culture.

1. Power to transcend paradigms. While being able to change paradigms is powerful, even more powerful is the ability to "stay above" paradigms—to recognize that they are constructs, not "truth." This allows you then to choose paradigms that best suit your purpose. Donella Meadows summed up the characteristics of this leverage point quite well in her article.[17]

> It is to "get" at a gut level the paradigm that there are paradigms, and to see that that itself is a paradigm, and to regard that whole realization as devastatingly funny. It is to let go into Not Knowing, into what the Buddhists call enlightenment. . . . It is in this space of mastery over paradigms that people throw off addictions, live in constant joy, bring down empires, get locked up or burned at the stake or crucified or shot, and have impacts that last for millennia.

(And if I go any further, we will get into the territory of philosophy . . .)

As you move along these leverage points from 12 to 1, notice how their characteristics go from physical (points 12 to 10), to informational (points 9 to 6), to social (points 5 to 3), to conscious (points 2 and 1). The least effective changes we can make are smaller, physical changes within the system itself, such as tax rates or subsidies. Not coincidentally, these changes are the easiest to effect and are often the types of changes modern politics is concerned with. However, if a change at this level is material enough that it affects lower-numbered items, it may be somewhat more effective. Keep in mind as well that this ranking is general, not precise.

Let us consider the medical system in the United States as an example to move through these leverage points. One of the main problems in the US is the exorbitant cost of healthcare with macro-level results that are not as good as many other developed countries. How could we solve this?

Starting in the realm of weakest leverage points, we could subsidize hospitals (leverage point 12) or simply build more of them (leverage point 11); those changes might alleviate some pressure but are unlikely to eliminate the problem. We could try to change structures or operations within the hospital system, such as the design of the hospitals themselves, or the process by which patients are treated (leverage point 10), and some of these changes might also reduce delays in some areas (leverage point 9); however, many problems would likely remain.

We could also increase the strength of negative feedback loops (leverage point 8), which in this case are things that would promote public health, such as promotion and availability of healthy food options, regular exercise, and making time for rest and rejuvenation. On the opposite side, we could turn up the gain on doctors and hospitals and the medical industry, and keep throwing more money, people, time, and resources at the situation, increasing everything about it in a general sense (leverage point 7)—in other words, *more* of the same solutions.

Another solution would be to provide greater feedback to the population about their health (leverage point 6) and the dire consequences of unhealthy choices. This could be accomplished by various means, such as regular testing and bloodwork, daily weigh-ins, or wearing a health-tracking device such as a Fitbit. Anything that lets us keep track of our health and monitor it more closely may help accomplish this goal.

Alternatively, we could implement rules or punishments (leverage point 5) for people who are overweight or unhealthy, such as fines or insurance premium increases. We could tax certain foods, try to control what people eat, dictate how much they exercise, and how often they see the doctor, via all kinds of rules and enforcement procedures—although we might also end up with a lot of stressed-out, unhappy people (and possibly a black market for Twinkies). Additionally, issues with privacy, discrimination, freedom, human rights, and equality often surface with these sorts of tactics.

Bernie Sanders managed to inspire a large voter base by proposing we reorganize the healthcare system (at least partially) by reducing or eliminating profit as the goal (leverage point 4), and creating a much more powerful shared goal (leverage point 3)—Medicare for All. If the purpose of providing healthcare is profit, the system will likely keep functioning as it is. If the purpose shifts to promoting and maintaining health and wellness for all (and profits exit stage left), that change in purpose promotes change in all the higher-numbered leverage points— taxes, subsidies, health networks, incentives, punishments, and so on. Many of those items would get restructured due to the nature of the more fundamental change within the system. This demonstrates exactly why strong leverage points are so effective in creating change; by necessity, they often change many aspects of related systems at the same time.

In our healthcare system, there is a paradigm that we should pay for medical services because it requires vast amounts of money, time, and resources for medical professionals to go to school, for hospitals and care providers to tend to patients, for expensive research and equipment, for salaries and buildings and rent and food and more. The prevailing mindset is something like "If you get sick, you should pay for your care; if you are lucky enough to not get sick, you get to retain more of your wealth." An alternate mindset or paradigm (leverage point 2) would be that access to healthcare is a fundamental right and every human being should have access to the healthcare they need without worrying about going bankrupt or not being able to pay their rent. Additionally, we could adopt the paradigm that our environment, work lives, and social structures can and should be engineered to promote the overall health, well-being, and happiness of the general population, which would reduce the need and demand on the healthcare system overall.

Exercising the strongest leverage point in our healthcare example would be conceding that the capitalist model of healthcare can no longer sustainably serve humanity, and then being willing to easily, happily, and readily change that paradigm (as well as any organizational structures).

THINKING IN SYSTEMS

As a society, if we could transcend the profit/growth mindset that surrounds the monetary system, we would go from a paradigm of competition and consumerism to a paradigm of cooperation and reverence for nature and fellow humans, with a purpose of achieving a sustainable balance between economy and ecology. We could shift our thinking from having to be compensated directly for every single task we perform, to knowing that there are enough resources for everyone and that if we all cooperate and work together, no single person needs to trade their time or labor to have their needs met. We could go from a mindset and belief system that equates success and happiness with zeros in a bank account or the size and number of homes we own, to a system that equates happiness and success with contribution, relationships, wisdom, sustainability, empathy, and community. This is the type of root, systemic, paradigm-transcending change that we hope will take hold in the coming years and decades, and the type of change, with all its possibilities, that we will be discussing throughout the second part of this book.

As we explore ideas and concepts, I encourage you to think about all the systems involved in different aspects of our day-to-day lives, and about how many of them revolve around the monetary system. Think about how many activities, habits, and institutions are constructs created by the current economic system, and how many of them offer little humanitarian value to the world—or, worse, cause damage. The more we can look at all the interconnections, feedback loops, and strong leverage points, the more we can begin to see the unnecessary detrimental activity within our monetary system and how it makes the rest of the world revolve around it. The more we see these relationships and how different systems interact, the more we can visualize alternatives to the current system, and the more we can begin to build and live them in our own lives. And this is the beginning of true change, for both us and the world.

CHAPTER 3

THE PROBLEM WITH PROFIT

When wealth is passed off as merit, bad luck is seen as bad character. This is how ideologues justify punishing the sick and the poor. But poverty is neither a crime nor a character flaw. Stigmatize those who let people die, not those who struggle to live.

SARAH KENDZIOR, JOURNALIST, AUTHOR, ANTHROPOLOGIST

Now that we have some grounding in systems thinking, let's look at a few of the systems in place so we can understand how the market economy and the profit motive inherently create conditions of scarcity, poverty, homelessness, and many other difficult-to-address societal and economic issues. We will look at four systems that provide a good representation of the economy as a whole: the labor market, the housing market, the healthcare system, and the industrial sector.

By diagramming how a system functions and examining causal loops, we can better understand why the system gets the results it does and identify common patterns. We will show only primary relationships in these diagrams; other relationships certainly exist, but including them in the diagrams complicates things more than necessary. Our goal is not to list all the things that are wrong, but to expose the underlying systems that cause major problems, to portray the primary relationships and feedback loops between profit and different sectors of our economy, and to highlight the range of results they produce. We will detail more of the real-world effects of these systems in the next chapter.

THE LABOR MARKET

In terms of the effects of the monetary system, the one thing that most people reading this book can easily relate to is the pressure to "get a job"—to sell their time and effort in some form or fashion to afford the necessities of life. And if there is a single piece of the monetary puzzle that people would like to see eliminated more than any other, it would be this never-ending struggle that many of us endure daily to work, pay our bills, and survive.

Let us begin with the basic idea of a market economy and what could loosely be termed "capitalism." In Figure 3 we have a causal loop diagram with four elements: *labor*, *surplus*, *profit*, and *means of production*, each with an arrow leading clockwise to the next.

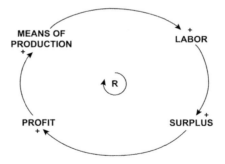

Figure 3: Causal Loop Diagram of Market Economy

Notice all the arrows have plus signs by them, meaning that a change in one leads to a corresponding change in the next. In each of these relationships, if one item increases, the next increases; if one item decreases, the next decreases. Thus, it is a reinforcing feedback loop, as indicated by the "R" in the circular arrow in the center.

To understand what this diagram means in a practical sense, as an example let us use a farm on which we grow corn. We start with the things we own, such as land, tools, and seeds, which are the *means of production*. Then we put in some *labor*—that is, we sow and harvest our corn crop. After we take enough corn to feed ourselves, pay our expenses, and plant another crop next year, whatever is left over is the *surplus*. We can sell the surplus to make a *profit*. With the profit, we can invest in more land or tools, thus further increasing the means of production, and the loop begins again. More land and more tools generally mean more labor waiting to be done, which leads to even more surplus, and so on. This model of creating surplus and reinvesting the profits from that surplus is the foundation of practically any business that has experienced any growth at all.

Notice that this is a very simple model and that our example ignores at least one big system factor: weather. We might use our means of production and put in the labor, but if there is a drought, we may not have any surplus. If surplus decreases, profit decreases, and, depending on investors, subsidies, and other factors, means of production may or may not decrease, and the need for labor the following season may or may not decrease, as well. I point this out just as a reminder that all models are "false" because life is much more complex than our models could ever be. Nonetheless many models are still useful.

Let us say that after we (the farm owners) have made some significant profits, we decide to purchase more land and tools and hire a few workers. We pay an acceptable rate for the work, average for the area. The additional labor and increased means of production give us the opportunity to produce a much greater surplus than we could have produced on our own.

We now have a choice: share the profits with the workers, or keep the profits for ourselves. If we are kindly and good-hearted, perhaps we will share the profits. However, we are rather typical business owners and instead of sharing the additional wealth that the surplus generates, we decide to keep most of it for ourselves, while reinvesting a portion back into the business and thus repeating the cycle of profit and growth.

As the farm owners, we have now acquired additional profits and increased means of production. This means we have a business arrangement in which we, the business owners, receive more money than the workers do. This unequal allocation creates a gap between our wealth and the wealth the workers possess. In other words, *inequality* is born of this relationship designed for owners to benefit from workers' labor.

Additionally, now that we have accumulated more wealth and more means of production than the workers have, we also have an economic advantage when it comes to further expanding our means of production and acquiring even more wealth. When it comes to starting or expanding a business endeavor, we are in a far better situation than most of our workers. As time goes on and our advantage in wealth, assets, and opportunity expands, it will be increasingly difficult for any of our workers to compete with us.

This pattern where, essentially, the rich get richer is a classic example of the archetype mentioned earlier known as *success to the successful*, which occurs when those with an economic advantage can use that advantage to create more profits, while simultaneously reinforcing conditions in which those without that advantage receive a continually shrinking share of the overall wealth over time. In this archetype, the gap between the advantaged and the disadvantaged, the owners and the workers, the wealthy and the poor is reinforced and widened over time.

To illustrate this archetype in a causal loop diagram, in Figure 4 we keep most of our original loop on the right to represent our already-wealthy business owners, and we add a new loop on the left to represent the workers, which will contain *resources*, *education and opportunities*, and *wages/earnings*. *Profit* is a shared point where the two loops meet, and *allocation of resources to the owners/wealthy* is added as another shared point to show how resources are diverted from workers and instead end up going to the owners.

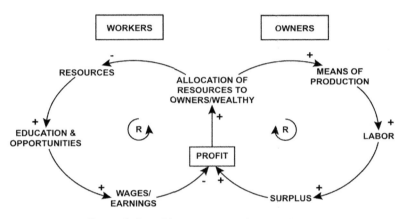

Figure 4: Causal Loop Diagram of Labor Market

First off, notice that in the left-hand loop, there are two minus signs. Recall that, as in multiplication, two negatives cancel each other out to equal a positive, which means both this cycle and the right-hand cycle (with all plusses) create reinforcing feedback loops. That means that unless something interrupts the cycle, the gap between workers and owners will continue to grow, as we are witnessing today.

In reading our left-hand loop, let us start with *profit* and move counterclockwise. If profit increases, this generally increases the *allocation of resources to owners/wealthy*, since business owners (or

CEOs/upper management) receive most of the profits, which can in turn be used to pay for resources. When more resources go to the owners, proportionally fewer *resources* go to workers, as illustrated in the diagram by the minus sign.

Resources increase the chances of having more and better *education and opportunities*. However, since the communities where workers live receive fewer resources, people in these communities often have less education and fewer opportunities. Because wealthier people can pay for more resources while those with less money cannot, resources that could have fostered growth and development in less-wealthy communities (and enabled them to better compete in the marketplace) go to wealthier people and communities instead. As a result, less privileged communities typically have less education funding, less job training, and less access to capital for startups.

When *education and opportunities* abound, *wages/earnings* generally increase, as shown by the plus sign in the diagram. However, when *resources* are scarce, *education and opportunities* decrease, leading to decreasing *wages/earnings* for people in lower-income communities. Lastly, in our left-hand loop, with all else being equal, the wealthy owners get to keep (proportionally) more of the *profits* for themselves, thus beginning the cycle again.

Many people intuitively understand these dynamics to a degree, but drawing it out in a causal loop diagram is helpful because it makes one thing clear: this is a systemic relationship that has been around since the beginnings of capitalism; the business owners depend on a class of people who need jobs to pay their bills and survive. The workers have little means to sustain themselves without selling their labor, which provides the labor machine for the wealthier capitalists. If workers had enough land and resources to sustain themselves, they would likely not submit to laboring in return for wages. In other words, the workers' lack of resources is one of the central mechanisms of how the wealthy acquire more resources.[18]

This diagram is, of course, just a diagram and cannot illustrate the spectrum of conditions that various individuals and communities fall under; there are differing degrees of control over one's employment status, and there is a range of wealth and poverty between one community and the next. However, this diagram effectively illustrates the *systemic* relationship between workers and the owners by exemplifying the ever-widening wealth gap we see commonly exhibited throughout the world today.

Now let us look at another system that is closely related to labor: housing.

THE HOUSING MARKET

Income is one of the biggest determinants of where we live and what kind of housing we can access. Here in the United States, there is a glut of high-end housing (a large portion of which often sits empty) and a lack of quality low-cost housing. How does this happen?

To see the systemic relationships behind this, let us look at Figure 5. In this diagram, we can see how the feedback loops in our housing system, with low-cost homes on the left and high-cost homes on the right, create another example of the success-to-the-successful archetype. (Incidentally, this is another example of how simple models can be useful in understanding system dynamics without needing to incorporate all the detail of, say, the middle-class development that would not be labeled "high-cost" or "low-cost" development. Housing certainly exists along a spectrum.)

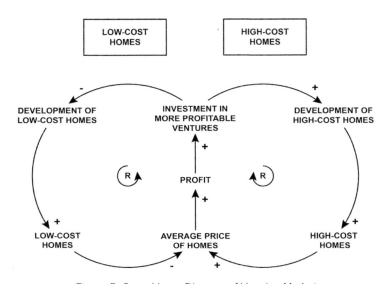

Figure 5: Causal Loop Diagram of Housing Market

Let us start at *investment in more profitable ventures*, a shared point in the two loops, and move clockwise around the right-hand loop. Since homebuilders are generally looking to make the most money from their investments and since luxury homes tend to have the highest returns, homebuilders often seek to build higher-end housing within a given area. Therefore, when resources are allocated to the most profitable ventures, this results in an increase in the *development of high-cost homes*. From there, it is not difficult to see that the incentive to develop high-cost homes leads to an increase in the number (the stock) of *high-cost homes*.

The more high-cost homes are built in an area, the more the *average price of homes* (another shared point in the two loops) in that area tends to rise. Higher average prices usually result in greater amounts of *profit*, a third shared point, which, again, leads to more *investment in more profitable ventures*. Thus, more high-end properties are developed, in a repeating cycle of increasingly higher-cost housing. The "R" in the circular arrow indicates this is a reinforcing cycle.

Now let us look at the left-hand loop. Starting at the top and moving counterclockwise, when there is *investment in more profitable ventures,* the proportion of resources available for the *development of low-cost homes* decreases. When fewer resources are put toward developing low-cost homes, fewer *low-cost homes* are built. The less affordable housing there is available in an area (that is, the lower the stock), the higher the *average price of homes* tends to be. Higher prices also drive lower-income people out of the neighborhood, which further eliminates downward pressure on price (this sort of development process is also known as *gentrification*). As the average price rises, profit rises, and the cycle repeats.

Because of these dynamics, we see a lot of properties being improved upon and made more expensive. However, not many properties are built or improved more economically in order to remain less expensive. This leads to overdevelopment for the rich, who can pay the higher premiums, and underdevelopment for those with lower incomes. Also, because there is an over-supply of homes for the wealthy, their affluence often means they own multiple houses. The technical term for this is *hoarding*—that is, the practice of collecting or accumulating more than is needed.

As a result, we have created a situation of artificial scarcity and a wasteful misallocation of resources. In 2020, the US had over 580,000 homeless people[19] and 13.6 *million* vacant housing units[20]—about twenty-three units per homeless person. At the same time, older, less-expensive structures that could be reno-vated for use by lower-income residents are torn down com-pletely to make way for higher-cost housing. Similarly, "flippers" buy homes not to live in them but to make improvements so they can "flip" them for profit—driving up surrounding prices and sometimes netting hundreds of thousands of dollars on a single sale. Eventually, many older, once reasonably affordable neighborhoods become increasingly accessible only to high-income earners, while millions of low-income buyers continue to struggle to simply find affordable housing—let alone actually *buy* a home.

Let us now turn to another industry that continues to put profits before people in numerous ways: healthcare.

THE HEALTHCARE SYSTEM

In 2020, nearly 20 percent of the entire GDP of the United States was spent on healthcare.[21] That means that almost one out of every five dollars spent in America is spent on the medical system. Even though we spend more money per capita on healthcare than any other nation (by far), we somehow still rank only twenty-seventh on the list of healthcare systems by country—down from sixth in 1990.[22] In fact, the United States comes in dead last for outcomes among high-income countries—and happens to be the *only* country on that list without universal healthcare.[23]

The US healthcare system is so convoluted that we could easily write an entire chapter (if not an entire book) about it to consider moving targets like insurance, drugs, marketing, the food industry, and so on. However, it is not necessary to take a deep dive to understand the basic relationships and dynamics underlying the inherent dysfunction in the system. To illustrate this dysfunction, Figure 6 is a diagram illustrating two common feedback loops. This diagram is another example of the success-to-the-successful archetype, where the least-profitable ventures or solutions are not developed or supported. We have *low-cost/*

free treatments on the left and *profitable treatments* on the right with two shared points: *profit* and *investment in more profitable treatments.*

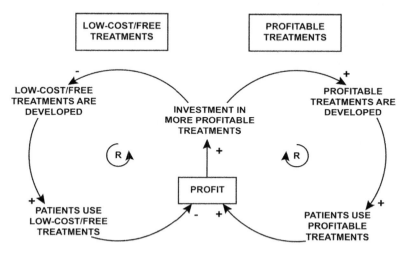

Figure 6: Causal Loop Diagram of Healthcare System

Let's start again with *profit* and travel clockwise around the right-hand loop. When profits are made and then reinvested, they are typically allocated to the projects that maximize returns. This is indicated in the diagram by showing that when *profit* increases, the *investment in more profitable treatments* increases. When resources are allocated toward profitable ventures, then more *profitable treatments are developed.* When we get more development of profitable treatments, this translates to an increase in the number of *patients using profitable treatments,* which thereby increases the amount of *profit.* At that point we are back at the beginning, where the profits are invested again, and businesses undergo further expansion and development. Once again, the cycle repeats itself in a positive feedback loop, as indicated by the "R" in the circular arrow.

However, as will be no surprise by now, as we travel counter-clockwise in the left-hand loop, we can see that when *profit* is realized and more money is put toward *investment in more profitable treatments,* proportionally fewer dollars and resources go into the development of low-cost/free solutions, so fewer *low-cost/free treatments are developed.* This includes not only things like free clinics or hospitals, but also things that lead to better health outcomes, such as free or low-income housing, parks, gyms, recreational facilities, childcare, paid parental leave, in-home postpartum care, neighborhood gardens, nutritious food options, relationship counseling, education, shorter working hours, and so on.

When these types of solutions are developed and implemented, more *patients use low-cost/free solutions.* When people take advantage of free and low-cost systems and treatments to manage their health and well-being, it reduces the dependence on the for-profit healthcare system and translates into a decrease in overall profits. This is indicated by the minus sign pointing to *profit* on the left-hand side of the diagram. However, because these solutions are not developed or available to many people, by default many individuals are forced to use the for-profit healthcare system, which leads to an increase in profits and further reinforcement of that system.

Let us note that while many elements in the healthcare system are nonprofit, proportionally many more are for-profit. As a result of the overall profit-driven nature of the system, even the nonprofit elements often act as though they are for-profit. And because of the overall for-profit structure, the healthcare system does not and *cannot* provide the level of systemic repair needed to adequately address the societal dysfunction that manifests as diseases, addictions, or other mental and physical disorders.

Instead of preventing diseases in the first place by allowing and helping people to achieve a quality of life that brings about optimal health and wellness, our profit-driven system tends to impede a healthy lifestyle, while capitalizing on the opportunity to diagnose and treat patients with the latest drugs and technology—at a premium price. However, to achieve optimal health, or even to simply *maintain* health, often what we most need are lifestyle changes, a healthful environment, taking on less work or stress, leaving abusive relationships, maintaining dietary/fitness habits, access to community resources, and so on. And often, money has an enormous part to play in these circumstances. In fact, money is such a determinant of health and wellness that a 2020 study found wealthy people over the age of fifty generally live seven to nine more healthy years than low-income people over age fifty.[24]

Many corporations attempt to address some of these things via philanthropy or promotion of self-care within the workplace, but the scope and effectiveness of their efforts are relatively limited due to the constraints that the monetary system produces. The most employers can usually do to address individuals' or communities' health issues is to simply pay their employees more or provide affordable, adequate health insurance. Ideally, doing so will grant those wage earners access (financially) to more health-sustaining resources. Rarely, however, do companies go out of their way to improve conditions within communities themselves, since there is generally no direct profit realized from such activities.

Next, we look at the industrial sector, which, as with our healthcare system, gives decision-makers few incentives to improve conditions in their surrounding communities.

THE INDUSTRIAL SECTOR

Within the industrial sector, we include manufacturing, agriculture, energy, and so on. When it comes to the industrial sector (as well as most other sectors, really), what is most sustainable is often the least profitable. The opposite generally holds true as well: what is most profitable is often the least sustainable. This is because sustainable, solution-oriented production will generally produce the fewest number of items possible, transport them the least, and minimize resource expenditure in the process. Unfortunately, the capitalist system tends to encourage the opposite.

Let us illustrate this dynamic by again using—you guessed it—a causal loop diagram. In Figure 7, on the left, we have ventures geared toward *sustainable production*. On the right, we have ventures geared toward *profitable production*.

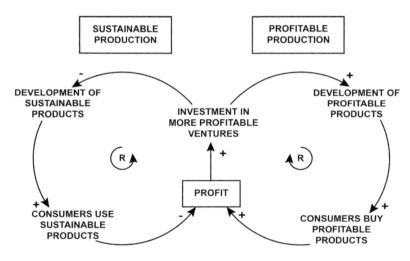

Figure 7: Causal Loop Diagram of Industrial Sector

You can see, once again, how the success-to-the-successful archetype plays out in this scenario, with the most profitable ventures growing and reinforcing themselves, while the least profitable (and typically most sustainable) ventures receive less development or promotion (which also happens to reinforce the most profitable ventures as well). Of course, sustainability and profitability need not be mutually exclusive, and the degree to which they correlate runs along a spectrum, but since the current system reinforces profit, it's often difficult for business owners to choose sustainability without being accused of not serving their shareholders' best interest.

With that in mind, let us look at how a typical scenario functions.

We will start with *profit*, a shared point in the middle of the diagram, and move clockwise around the right-hand loop. We already know that business owners typically invest in ventures that maximize returns (profits). Hence, when profits are made, this increases the amount of *investment in more profitable ventures*, a second shared point. When the amount of money and resources allocated toward profitable ventures increases, the *development of profitable products* increases as well. With the subsequent manufacturing and marketing of these products and services, the effect is that more *consumers buy profitable products*. The more of these high-profit, resource-intensive goods and services consumers buy, the more this maximizes *profit*, which brings us back to the beginning of the cycle.

Looking at the left side of the diagram and moving counterclockwise, when profits are generated and thus positively affect *investment in more profitable ventures*, proportionally fewer resources are dedicated to the *development of sustainable products*. When these free/low-profit, low-impact projects are developed and promoted, more consumers seek them out. However, since the profit incentive reduces the development and promotion of these options (as illustrated by the first negative sign in the left-hand loop), the effect is fewer *consumers use sustainable products*.

All else being equal, the use of free or low-cost sustainable products generally reduces profits from the high-profit, resource-intensive versions of those products. But because fewer sustainable products are available, fewer consumers use them and thus a greater portion buy the profitable products, thereby increasing profits. Because of the two negatives on the sustainable side of the diagram, both sides of the diagram are reinforcing cycles (note the "R" in the circular arrow on each side), thus exacerbating the gap between the two, much like we saw in the labor and housing markets.

Let us list a few examples of how and why these dynamics play out in such a fashion. For instance, a single ceramic plate could last a lifetime if cared for. Over the same duration, we could use many thousands of paper plates. In this scenario, the paper plate company stands to make much more money than the ceramic plate company if it were to serve the same number of customers for the same amount of time. However, there would be a significant increase in resource usage to manufacture and deliver millions of paper plates over the course of many years.

Another good example comes from the automotive industry. It would be very profitable for manufacturers if everyone on the planet owned a gas-guzzling SUV (or three), and if everyone drove a lot. However, with more sustainable options, such as walking (and developing walkable cities), cycling, ride-/vehicle-sharing, and using affordable/free mass-transit powered by renewable energy, we would eliminate a significant portion of those potential profits.

Capitalism also incentivizes transporting resources across the globe to be processed by workers who can be paid a fraction of what labor costs in the United States, and then transporting finished items back to the US consumer market. You can see this in products like a plastic-packed, snack-size serving of peaches. The peaches could be grown in Argentina, processed in the Philippines, then shipped to the United States for sale and consumption. Practices like this use massive amounts of resources and are in no way sustainable in the long term.

Lastly, sustainability tends to decrease when more commercial elements are added to the production and processing of an item. For instance, if you grow a tomato in your backyard using rainwater, and then eat that tomato fifty feet away at your kitchen table, it is not a very resource-intensive process. However, if a tomato is produced at a factory farm and ends up on your kitchen table, the process requires commercial farm equipment, transportation, labeling, accounting, marketing, and more—all requiring additional resources and energy input.

Unfortunately, all this intensive resource and energy use does not come without its consequences.

EXTERNALITIES, BALANCING LOOPS & CRISIS

While the details of individual sectors and systems certainly vary, a common pattern is shared. In general, as has been the recurring theme, when profits are made and business owners reinvest those profits back into their businesses, they generally tend to allocate them toward the development of more high-profit, resource-intensive products, without regard to the externalities that might be occurring in conjunction with their company's growth. (Remember, *externalities* are outside effects or consequences not reflected in the price.)

In the labor market, a notable externality is the millions of people who have no choice but to work long hours, often at monotonous, stressful, or even dangerous jobs, simply to survive. The lack of low-income housing creates the externality of a large unhoused population. In our healthcare system, the externalities include millions of sick and/or bankrupt people. In the industrial sector, we have the externalities of resource depletion, pollution, and climate change, to name a few.

As we have noted, this approach cannot continue forever. Because of the nature of our planet and environment, runaway reinforcing feedback loops will inevitably be interrupted when outside forces balance them out. Two such forces are already starting to disrupt our society and economy—climate change and social unrest. Let us explore these issues now for a moment, and then we will come back to them in greater detail in the next chapter.

In Figure 8, we have a diagram that illustrates the feedback loops that have been surfacing in our society and environment as of late.

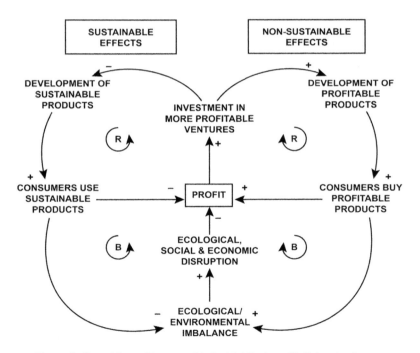

Figure 8: Causal Loop Diagram of Industrial Sector with Balancing Loops

We have kept the original double-loop diagram from the industrial section, and we have added a section to the bottom with two more loops to illustrate how business-as-usual will eventually be limited and disrupted by ecological, social, and economic problems. *Profit* is the shared point for all four loops.

When examining the right-hand side of this extended diagram (the non-sustainable effects), we can now see that when *consumers buy profitable products*, not only does this increase *profit*, but this also increases the level of *ecological/environmental imbalance* (bottom right loop). Our society relies on the environment to provide us with things like food, water, energy, and raw materials. When any of these factors begins to slide toward an unbalanced state, it threatens the stability of our socioeconomic system overall, which increases the level of *ecological, social, and economic disruption*. We can see these disruptions in the forms of climate change, resource overshoot, the COVID-19 pandemic, wildfires, floods, climate refugees, overfishing, droughts, crop failures, famines, civil unrest, and the supply chain crises. These types of disruptions generally affect *profit* in a negative way. Therefore, this bottom-right loop is a balancing loop (noted by the letter "B" in the circular arrow in the center) that is acting against the force of profit. What's more, as time goes on, these disruptions will worsen and this balancing loop will become stronger.

In the opposite vein, on the bottom left-hand side (the sustainable effects), we can see that when *consumers use sustainable products*, it lessens *ecological/environmental imbalance*, which in turn lessens *ecological, social, and economic disruption*. While the profit incentive still works against sustainability, this loop is a force that works against the profit motive. It will strengthen as time passes and more sustainable alternatives to products become available and more disruptions continue to decrease profits (and subsequently lower society's overall opinion of the importance of investing in profitable ventures). Also note that there are now three minus signs in the outer left-hand loop (that is, the loop on the left that goes around both the top and bottom), and one minus sign in the outer right-hand loop. Because there is an odd number of minus signs in each outer loop, these are both *balancing feedback loops*, meaning they will counteract the effects of the positive feedback loops in various ways.

Furthermore, this diagram illustrates that one way for us to prevent the loop of imbalance and disruption from wreaking havoc on our society is to use sustainable alternatives (as well as regenerative practices, which we will cover in Part Two of this book). These actions will enable us to lessen greenhouse gas emissions, sequester carbon, curtail resource overshoot, reduce pollution, restore our environment, and address social unrest and inequality.

We could draw many more causal loop diagrams and highlight dozens or even hundreds of externalities, such as the lack of proper infrastructure maintenance, shorter lifespans, and a consumer culture driven by a marketing industry that exploits the numerous voids in our lives to sell us things we don't need. Additionally, many of these externalities combine and overlap, playing off one another and compounding their effects.

We've looked at how profit drives our systems toward certain predictable results. By now, similar patterns in other systems should be easily recognizable. Let's extend our discussion into exploring some additional common patterns and consequences that come about because of our highly competitive growth- and profit-driven socioeconomic system.

CHAPTER 4

THE CONSEQUENCES
OF CAPITALISM

When the last tree is cut, the last fish is caught, and the last
river is polluted; when to breathe the air is sickening, you will
realize, too late, that wealth is not in bank accounts and that
you can't eat money.

ALANIS OBOMSAWIN, DOCUMENTARY FILMMAKER

In 2015, photographs of the body of two-year-old Alan Kurdi, soaked and lying face-down on a beach, rocked the world. Alan, along with his mother and five-year-old brother, drowned after their boat capsized as they attempted to flee from conflicts and resource shortages in Syria. The image of Alan, still wearing his red shirt, blue shorts, and tiny Velcro shoes, hit far too close to home for millions of people. The world erupted in an outpouring of support and cries for an end to the conflicts. Alan was one of more than twenty thousand people who died while crossing the Mediterranean in the European refugee crisis from 2014 to 2021.[25]

The conflicts in Syria that eventually led to thousands of refugees drowning at sea have now been linked to human-induced drought and climate change. Syria was part of the Fertile Crescent, where (we think) humans began practicing large-scale agriculture around 10,000 BCE. Most of the farmers in northern Syria depend on rain, which is now more infrequent and unpredictable. Droughts in the area used to occur on average every fifty-five years. That number is now every seven or eight years.[26] Millions of people who could no longer subsist on the land were forced to leave the parched countryside, prompting uprisings in surrounding areas with scarce, poorly managed resources. Subsequent armed conflicts resulted in a bloody civil war and sent nearly seven million people scrambling for their lives, seeking refuge in Turkey (now officially the Republic of Türkiye) and other countries. Jamal Saghir, professor at the Institute for the Study of International Development at McGill University said, "Syria serves as prime example for the impact of climate change on pre-existing issues such as political instability, poverty and scarce resources."[27]

The tens of thousands of unnecessary deaths that occurred in the Syrian refugee crisis are also an example of what is called *structural violence*. Structural violence occurs when any action or consequence of actions, systems, or social structures causes harm to, oppresses, or creates a barrier for a person or persons to reach their full potential. Structural violence can be overt or covert, and it manifests in countless ways. Practically all the negative effects of capitalism can be considered forms of structural violence. Syria is just one of many examples of the social, economic, and ecological disruptions that are already plaguing our society.

When we understand how systems in our society, economy, and environment work and interact, it becomes easier to see how problems are created and then spiral into scenarios that originally might seem completely unrelated. Because of the nature of feedback loops and the inherent delays between causes and effects, sometimes the ramifications of our actions take years or even decades to materialize.

Here I want to bring to light some of the most notable examples of how these scenarios play out, which will help us begin to see these patterns and feedback loops in the world around us. I would like to emphasize, however, that the number, scope, and complexity of the externalities and consequences we face as both a society and a species far exceed the space available in this book.

INEQUALITY

Capitalism creates and even incentivizes massive inequality throughout the world in endless ways—food deserts, poor education opportunities, police brutality, freeways built in places that intentionally separate communities. The ways in which inequality manifests are diverse and multitudinous.

As we repeatedly illustrated in the last chapter, and as you can likely already guess, the main cause behind inequality today is the profit motive, along with the competition and hoarding that our economic structure incentivizes. Humans possess the technology and resources to provide all necessities and more for every living person on the planet. As we saw, the market system prevents an equitable distribution of resources from occurring due to the incentive to invest in profitable ventures and the tendency to avoid projects that do not generate a quantifiable monetary return on investment. Two of the most striking ways that inequality has manifested in our modern society are poverty and systemic racism.

POVERTY

Poverty can be defined as the lack of access to resources necessary to satisfy basic needs.[28] In less developed areas of the world, the definition often includes a lack of life-sustaining necessities, such as food, clean water, sanitation facilities, and shelter. In more developed areas, the definition may be extended to include a lack of things that are needed to function within society, such as reliable transportation, a computer, internet access, healthy food options, and an education.

Poverty is the largest unrecognized root cause of death in the world today, which also means it is the cause of the most structural violence and inequality in society. According to the UN, twenty-five thousand people die from hunger every day.[29] One out of every three people on the planet still lacks access to safe drinking water.[30] Every year, more people die from unsafe water than from war and all other forms of physical violence.[31] These forms of poverty are all problems that are fixable with the technology we possess today. That these problems still exist is primarily a matter of the inequality and subsequent poverty that are inevitable side effects of the profit motive.

Homelessness is a form of poverty that can have disastrous effects upon people's lives. According to the Institute for Children, Poverty & Homelessness (ICPH), homelessness has been shown to be linked to increased rates of domestic violence, deteriorating physical and mental health, food insecurity, substance abuse, and contraction of HIV/AIDS.[32] The tally of more than a half million homeless people in the United States is especially sad, since there are multiple vacant homes in the US for every single homeless person sleeping on the streets, in a tent, under a bridge, or in their car. To add insult to injury, experts have estimated that roughly one quarter of homeless people are employed and simply don't make enough money to afford a home in the city in which they live.[33]

As we noted in Chapter 1, to remain in business, companies must compete and grow. To do so, they must gain new customers, and one of the best ways to gain new customers is to sell the same things as other companies but for a lower price. Once the expenses related to land, building, material, and energy are negotiated as low as possible, the last piece left is the price of labor. Ultimately, lower wages and fewer jobs are the side effects of low-price competition.

Labor costs are generally reduced in one of three ways: reducing wages, outsourcing, and automation. When a factory closes and jobs are outsourced to other (typically cheaper) countries, it's like a game of musical chairs—some of the newly unemployed workers will find other jobs, but some will not, because there are fewer jobs to support the same population. The loss of wages in an area drives economic decline as people have less money to support the local economy. Likewise with automation: a few people might be needed to maintain the automated production lines, but usually some people will end up struggling to find employment.

Figure 9 illustrates the effects of these reductions, which is an example of the archetype known as *conflicting goals*. On one hand (the left-hand loop), the company would like to maximize profits and market share; on the other hand (the right-hand loop), most companies would also like to keep employees and pay them a good wage, so they can in turn invest in and develop their local communities. However, given the need for companies to stay competitive with one another, they often cannot satisfy both goals. Thus, they usually take actions that repeatedly affect both goals—one negatively and the other positively. The shared point of the two loops is—you guessed it—*company reduces labor costs*.

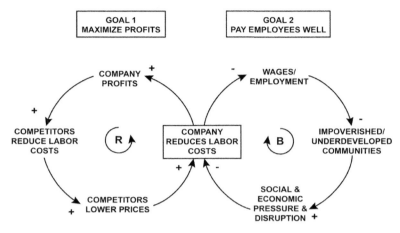

Figure 9: Causal Loop Diagram of Conflicting-Goals Archetype

In this diagram, to keep things simple, we will combine automation, outsourcing, and wage reduction together as forms of reducing labor costs. Starting in the middle and working counterclockwise around the left-hand loop, we can see that when a *company reduces labor costs*, it boosts *company profits* (Goal 1). Competitors see the first company's success, and to remain competitive, *competitors reduce labor costs*. Then in an attempt to gain market share, *competitors lower their prices*. When competitors reduce their prices enough, this forces the first company to reduce its labor costs even more, and the cycle repeats itself.

On the other side of the diagram beginning again from the middle and moving clockwise around the right-hand loop, you can see that when a *company reduces labor costs*, it directly lowers *wages/employment*. When there are lower wages and lower rates of employment in an area, it tends to lead to *impoverished/ underdeveloped communities.* Impoverished and underdeveloped communities tend to put a strain on both the immediate and surrounding communities and businesses. Crime, drugs, violence, decreasing property values, and so on can all contribute toward creating a downward spiral in social and economic activity in an area.

At this point, however, some pushback starts to happen in the form of *social and economic pressure and disruption*: the more impoverished communities become, the greater the pressure and disruption becomes. People begin to demand higher wages, they unionize, they strike—whatever it takes to be paid enough to earn a fair wage and stay out of poverty. This situation creates a balancing loop that acts against the reinforcing loop, which is why, if you happen to live in the United States, you likely have heard the demand for products that are "Made in America." Businesses have outsourced so many jobs to overseas workers that a good portion of the United States' once-mighty manufacturing economy has been gutted. However, even though many businesses would like to supply more jobs within the US, they now have no choice but to keep outsourcing much of their labor overseas for no other reason than to stay competitive with their prices.

The region of the United States known as the Rust Belt exemplifies this situation perfectly. This corridor, which stretches from the Midwest to the Northeast, used to be one of the largest manufacturing regions in the world. After countless jobs went to overseas manufacturers, the region became home to widespread deindustrialization, economic decline, poverty, population loss, and urban decay. A report by the Manhattan Institute, *Rust Belt Cities and Their Burden of Legacy Costs*, examined ninety-six different cities in the region and found that *all of them* had seen a rise in poverty rates since 1970, and three-quarters of the cities had experienced population decline.[34] Many of these cities rank among the highest in the US for drug use and crime as well.

At this point, with a clear view of the long-term systemic effects of competition and subsequent wage-cutting, it becomes undeniable that competition and the reduction of labor costs end up creating poverty and massive inequality. It is also undeniable how economic and profit incentives have helped create and exacerbate the problem of systemic racism throughout the economic history of the United States.

SYSTEMIC RACISM

Many people think racism is something now largely confined to the history books; however, it is undeniable that this inherently violent rhetoric and mindset, formed and solidified in social and economic systems of the past, lives on today in countless ways—some of which are blatant and others extremely subtle. This divisive, disruptive, and counterproductive way of thinking and acting also shows up in many of today's systems and institutions, which in turn shape the future of every person as an individual and of society as a whole.

In the United States, racial inequality extends back hundreds of years, and while this inequality may be recognized, it has never been fully addressed or resolved. Systemic racism, discrimination, and structural violence exist for Indigenous peoples, people of African, Asian, Middle Eastern, and Latino/Hispanic background, and more—but to keep our discussion relatively straightforward, we will briefly examine how the attitudes and practices of racism toward Black people in the United States came to exist, and how this racial discrimination has manifested into institutions and structures that continue to perpetuate systemic inequality to this day. While the specific stories for other groups may differ, the systemic elements that perpetuate inequality are similar.

Racism as we know it today (and especially racism toward people of African descent in the United States) did not exist when the colonies were first settled on the eastern coast of North America in the early 1600s. The term *race* was originally used to refer to a group that one was connected with, such as in kinship. The modern meaning of *race* to refer to people by physical traits or appearance was a social construct that came about in the mid-1660s when White colonists began to adopt the idea arising from the European Enlightenment of scientific categorization. They began to categorize humans, essentially to support the idea that White people were superior to "subhuman" Africans and "savage" Indians. Ultimately, of course, this reasoning was used to justify slavery.[35]

In the first European settlements in the Americas, indentured servants, most of whom were White, constituted a large portion of the labor for growing and harvesting crops. The transatlantic slave trade was still in its infancy, and purchasing an enslaved person was often deemed not worth the expense, since many early settlers quickly died from disease. Therefore, in the early 1600s, it was common for Black slaves and White indentured servants to work alongside one another, to share residences, and even to intermarry and have families. To the early settlers, religion was viewed as more important than race, so if a husband and wife were both Christians, even interracial marriage was typically accepted.[36]

As time went on and the colonies grew, disease rates dropped and the need for labor multiplied. Owning enslaved people gradually became more cost-effective, rendering the practice of paying for indentured servants all but obsolete, and thus the slave trade grew in tandem with many large plantations in the Americas. Eventually, enslaved people performed most of the labor required to produce the early Southern capitalists' main commodity, cotton (which like wool—and not coincidentally—could travel long distances and not spoil). As Cornell history professor Edward Baptist details in his book *The Half Has Never Been Told*:[37]

> White enslavers were able to force enslaved African-American migrants to pick cotton faster and more efficiently than free people. Their practices rapidly transformed the southern states into the dominant force in the global cotton market, and cotton was the world's most widely traded commodity at the time, as it was the key raw material during the first century of the industrial revolution. The returns from cotton monopoly powered the modernization of the rest of the American economy.

As enslaved Blacks began to make up a large portion of the labor in various industries (with a concentration in sugar and cotton), a need to fabricate some sort of moral pacification for the act of enslaving of another person surfaced. White slave owners began to view themselves as a superior race, intentionally thinking of and treating enslaved people of color as a lesser species in an attempt to rationalize their behavior. To reinforce their beliefs in their own superiority, in the late 1600s, White slave owners began resorting to ever-increasing levels of segregation, hostility, violence, and depravity toward enslaved people of African descent. Fast forward a couple hundred years to after the Civil War and emancipation, and these now-magnified, openly hostile sentiments led to the Jim Crow laws, further segregation, and the formation of hate groups such as the KKK.

The forms and effects of systemic racism and discrimination in our current society are far too numerous to list in this text, but a small enumeration includes the facts that on average, African Americans:

- Are hired less frequently and paid less for the same jobs as Whites[38]
- Are more likely to lack quality education or job resources[39]
- Have a smaller chance of being admitted to top colleges or universities[40]
- Are more likely to be arrested and sent to prison[41] (and stay there longer[42])
- Are more likely to face disproportionate barriers when voting[43]
- Have higher infant mortality rates[44]
- Receive fewer health benefits[45]
- Live in underfunded communities[46] that are more prone to higher rates of crime, drug use, and single-parent homes[47]

The lasting racist sentiment and the inequality produced by the early US economy is truly a difficult situation to resolve under the current capitalist structure, given the constraints within the system. But recognizing that racism's root cause is *economic* and being able to see the cyclical cause-and-effect relationship between our modern capitalist system and the perpetuation of present-day systemic racism is a major step in combating the inequality still overwhelmingly present in our communities. It is also a guide to understanding how to ultimately *reverse* these effects. However, the systems that solve the problem cannot be the same systems that created the problem.

One of the most prominent examples of how an intended solution ends up backfiring is that of the United States' system of incarceration—and especially the waging of the "drug war" for the last fifty-odd years. In 2021, the US incarcerated approximately 2.1 million individuals, or 639 people per 100,000—which is by far the largest per capita incarceration rate of any

country in the world.[48] And as noted, there is a disproportionate impact on persons of color.

This practice of overly relying on the incarceration system
to mitigate crime and implement corrective actions not only
inflicts often irreparable damage to the lives and productive
capacities of the prisoners, but it also directs funds away from
their communities (which could have helped lift them out of
poverty and crime in the first place) and into the police and
prison systems or even into the private bank accounts of
corporations. This results in an example of the archetype
known as *fixes that fail*, as shown in Figure 10.

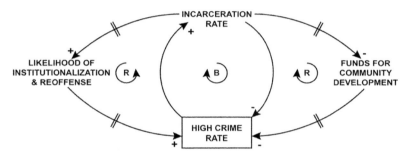

Figure 10: Causal Loop Diagram of Fixes-That-Fail Archetype (Incarceration)

In this diagram, we can see that at bottom center, we have
the initial problem of a *high crime rate*. To address this problem,
the traditional solution has been to arrest and incarcerate offenders. Therefore, when the crime rate increases, the *incarceration rate* (at the top of the diagram) generally increases as well.
Furthermore, as a superficial sign that the solution of incarceration is working (even if only temporarily), when the incarceration rate goes up, a reduction in the initial problem, the *high
crime rate*, comes to pass as well. This cycle is at the center of the
diagram and acts as a balancing loop, keeping the crime rate
somewhat low in the short term.

However, when we examine the longer-term side effects of incarceration, we can see that when the *incarceration rate* increases, because sending people to prison costs money, *funds for community development* (creating a new loop on the right) are reduced. When funding for community development is lacking, people don't have access to resources, education, or support systems. As a result, the crime rate typically increases, leaving us with the original problem of a *high crime rate*. This produces a reinforcing loop, which ultimately increases the crime rate even more, and more incarceration ensues, repeating the cycle.

Additionally, on the opposite side of the diagram, another side effect of incarceration is that once people go to prison, they experience a greater *likelihood of institutionalization and reoffense*. When we have a population that is more likely to commit repeat offenses, we are eventually led back to the same initial problem of a high crime rate. This left-hand loop is a reinforcing loop as well.

We have added one other aspect to this diagram that we have not included in previous illustrations—a delay in time, which is noted by the small double lines intersecting the arrows on the outsides of the diagram. This means that these side effects are not immediate; they take time to manifest. The delays portrayed in this justice system diagram generally occur over a period of months, years, or even decades. The fact that there is no immediate cause and effect to witness also makes it more difficult to pinpoint the relationships between these intersecting events. Because the two outer cycles are reinforcing feedback loops, and since one does not directly cause the other but instead manifests through a chain of events in the system, people often do not associate these types of causes with their eventual outcomes. Thus, as obvious as it may seem, we often miss the connection between things like a lack of community investment and a high crime rate.

It is also worth noting that taking limited actions, such as simply ending for-profit prisons, letting all nonviolent drug offenders go free, or stopping corporate use of prison labor, would not completely solve the problem of a high crime rate or mass incarceration. While each of these issues contributes to the overall problem and gives us insight into potential solutions, the main problem is that the "justice" system engages in the extreme overuse of incarceration and the avoidance of community-investment programs that would make a difference in the lives of the people who need them the most.

These programs are rarely funded because they do not provide fast enough or large enough returns on investment, or because they are erroneously seen as expenses with no benefit (or at least not enough benefit to those who pass the laws). Therefore, without the budget to properly implement sufficient social welfare programs in the United States, the government doesn't really have much of a choice *but* to mass incarcerate people (at least to some degree). Like the healthcare system, the justice system cannot adequately address the underlying root causes that lead to the symptomatic problems of drug use, violence, property crimes, and so on.[49] The legal, justice, and incarceration systems are simply too tied into the capitalist system, and they can each take only very limited measures due to budget and other decision-making constraints.

Interestingly enough—as we will detail more in Part Two of this book—when you consciously and intentionally fix the problems within our healthcare system, you simultaneously fix a large portion of the problems in the justice system. And inversely, *not* implementing solutions that address root causes produces numerous negative consequences in various aspects of people's lives.

We continue to see—repeatedly—that *everything is connected*.

RESOURCE OVERSHOOT

As we briefly discussed in Chapter 1, the term *resource overshoot* pertains to the overextraction and overuse of resources as well as to the amount of pollution and waste we put into our environment relative to the amount it can sustainably hold. In this regard, a pattern can be seen throughout history in which humans take too much from the earth without investing enough back into it. Scotland, which used to have huge forests but is now largely peatland, is a prime example of the consequences of deforestation. Whales are finally on the rebound after many species were nearly driven to extinction by whalers (good thing we started burning fossil fuels instead of whale oil . . . right?). Taking too much water from the ground without allowing the time for it to be replenished naturally (or building the infrastructure to assist in that process) is a problem that is becoming more and more widespread.

While resource overshoot has occurred in many relatively isolated instances around the world in the past, it is now catching up with us on a global scale.

The effects of our market economy's lack of attention to regeneration and renewal, combined with an incessant need for extraction and consumption, are exacerbated even further by a lack of monetary incentive to properly dispose of or repurpose our waste products. The unfortunate byproduct of this dysfunctional system is unfathomable amounts of garbage, toxic chemicals, food waste, obsolete electronics, old or broken consumer products, and plastic. Lots and lots of plastic . . . so much plastic that our oceans are swimming in it and our kids are peeing it out.[50] It is now to the point that if we are to survive in the long term, we literally cannot avoid cleaning up our mess any longer. It will take nothing short of a major overhaul in how we work, live, play, travel, grow our food, deliver items, and produce our energy to restore our planet's environment and start down a more sustainable path.

In this section we will discuss the most pressing aspects of resource overshoot: soil depletion and desertification, pollution and climate change, and, as a result of these overarching problems, an unprecedented loss of biodiversity throughout the world.

SOIL DEPLETION & DESERTIFICATION

Soil depletion occurs when the constituents that make up healthy soil are removed or destroyed and are not replenished. Healthy soil contains an entire ecosystem of bacteria, fungi, algae, protozoa, and other microorganisms. These tiny lifeforms interact with each other and provide a medium for the storage and transportation of the nutrients and minerals that plants need to grow and thrive. The ground we walk on is so dense with life that one spoonful of fresh, healthy soil can contain more microorganisms than we have people on the planet.[51]

Agriculture is often hailed as a godsend for humanity, enabling the birth of civilization and food production on the scale that made it possible to feed an ever-growing population. However, this technological innovation has not come without its price. With a focus on monoculture, increasing crop yields, and large-scale production, conventional agriculture (along with deforestation and overgrazing of animals) is a major contributor to climate change, soil depletion, and eventual desertification. Because of this, conventional agriculture, with all its machinery and chemicals, is a perfect example of a fix that has managed to work in the short term (for about the last eighty years, since World War II) but may not serve us in the long term. The chances of its maintaining ecological balance in the long run do not appear to be good. We are now learning the hard way that we must turn back to more holistically oriented systems to grow our food.

The unfortunate fact is that tilling the soil and using pesticides, fungicides, and herbicides without reinvestment of organic matter into the soil results in low-quality soil that then needs even more chemicals and fertilizers to make it relatively productive again. If nothing is done to restore the soil's natural, healthy ecology, these cycles result in soil degradation and eventual desertification. This has become such a problem that, at the rate we are currently degrading our topsoil, experts estimate that we will exhaust the farming capacity of our planet by the year 2080.[52] This is devastating news, of course, since we rely on topsoil to grow approximately 95 percent of our food.[53] This situation wouldn't be so incredibly hard to reverse if there were not massive infrastructure and incentives in place that support the practice of conventional agriculture; however, the monetary system and profit motive pose problems here as well. Let's look at how in Figure 11.

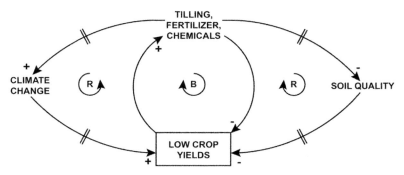

Figure 11: Causal Loop Diagram of Fixes-That-Fail Archetype
(Conventional Agriculture)

You'll notice that this diagram has a similar structure to the incarceration diagram, with a balancing loop in the center and a reinforcing loop with delayed effects to each side. Let's start at the bottom center with our problem, which is *low crop yields*. The fix that ultimately fails is the use of *tilling, fertilizer, and chemicals* ("chemicals" being a catchall for fungicides, pesticides, and so on). When these solutions are implemented, the problem of *low crop yields* is temporarily reduced, creating a balancing loop. However, we can also see that when we use *tilling, fertilizer, and chemicals* to increase crop yields, it produces two negative side effects—a reduction in *soil quality* (at right) and various greenhouse gas emissions that contribute to *climate change* (at left).

First, as illustrated to the right, *soil quality* is reduced because tilling, fertilizer, and chemicals destroy the microorganisms in the soil, making the soil quality lower in the long run. This, in turn, further reduces crop yields and increases dependency on tilling and using even more fertilizer and chemicals. Without the introduction of more organic matter in the soil to restore its health, we get a reinforcing cycle that results in a downward spiral of soil quality, eventually resulting in desertification.

On the left-hand side is the side effect of the emissions of greenhouse gases that contribute to *climate change*. Tilling practices disturb the top layer of soil and expose organic matter (made of carbon) to the oxygen in the air. Consequently, the carbon and oxygen react with one another, forming carbon dioxide and releasing greenhouse gases into the atmosphere. Additionally, fertilizers, pesticides, and other agricultural chemicals require a tremendous amount of energy and fossil fuels to produce, transport, and apply. Lastly, fertilizer runoff creates dead zones in the ocean; these result in massive algae blooms that suck all the oxygen out of the water, killing practically everything in the area. The hypoxic conditions also release nitrous oxide, a powerful greenhouse gas. (In another feedback loop not shown in the diagram, climate change also makes ocean dead zones worse, since warm water holds less oxygen and increases hypoxia. Additionally, increased frequencies and intensities of rainfall due to climate change mean more agricultural runoff ends up in the ocean.[54,55])

Unfortunately, our current economic system incentivizes this destructive cycle in the form of subsidies, grants, supply-chain dynamics, educational institutions, and more. The various legal, distribution, and economic systems combine and work in such a way that it becomes difficult for established farmers to adopt or transition to regenerative practices, and reliance on fossil fuels and chemicals is common in the industry. In the United States, about 20 percent of farmland is managed by no-till and/or regenerative practices,[56] which may seem like a lot, but we have a long way to go to make our agricultural practices sustainable for the long run, and the urgency cannot be overstated.

POLLUTION & CLIMATE CHANGE

Pollution is arguably the single most damaging and pressing issue we face regarding our collective survival, yet the problem only continues to escalate and magnify in nature. We could go on at length about the many types of pollution and their specific causes—the great Pacific garbage patch; the agricultural runoff that has caused over 400 dead zones in our oceans; everything from fracking chemicals to pharmaceuticals in the water; horrific air quality in many cities around the world; mountainous toxic landfills; microplastics found in both snow on top of the Alps and in our children's urine. This list is sobering, to say the least.

However, the effects of most forms of pollution pale in comparison to the long-term effects of the invisible, odorless pollutants that our vehicles and power plants emit continuously. The pollutants that society must immediately address, above any and all others, are greenhouse gas (GHG) emissions, which we all know by now produce the subsequent effect of climate change. Despite political and regulatory efforts to reduce emissions and restrict some ecologically destructive activities, many for-profit industries use money and power to manipulate the legal and political systems for their own benefit. Exxon conducted studies that proved greenhouse gas emissions were causing global warming all the way back in 1977—eleven years before it became a public issue.[57] Their findings were indisputable, yet they purposely concealed the studies and actively engaged in misinformation campaigns to confuse the public and slow change. Thus, the most insidious form of pollution persists, practically unchecked and with few signs of slowing, leading us into the beginning stages of anthropogenic (human-caused) climate change.

Climate change is a change in the average weather patterns of a region over time, and can include things like warming temperatures, increased or decreased rainfall, and more frequent extreme weather. While the phrase "climate change" may sound somewhat benign, humanity is teetering on the verge of nothing less than a mass-extinction event, not just for humans but possibly for most of the species on our planet. As time goes on, this picture will become clearer as inadequate efforts create a never-ending series of cascade effects and disruptions for our children and grandchildren. The increasing economic disruption and environmental devastation is already beginning to drown out the noise of those who continue to deny the science and stick to business as usual. Policymakers, sadly, have been slow to take effective action on cutting emissions and sequestering greenhouse gases.

There's also a real possibility that it's too late to stop catastrophic warming. We may have already triggered runaway feedback loops that will allow the release of even more greenhouse gases from permafrost melting, which releases more greenhouse gases, which then melts more permafrost . . . and the cycle repeats.

These "tipping points" also exist with sea ice melting, wildfires, and deforestation. The scary part is that we really don't know when these feedback loops become unstoppable, or whether they have already reached that point.

It is up to us to do everything we can to ensure we don't pass the point of no return. That means understanding the problem, and then doing everything we can to mitigate it. Let us briefly take a closer look at the systems that cause greenhouse gas emissions and climate change.

The most common sources of greenhouse gas emissions are:

- Burning of fossil fuels for transportation and energy—coal, oil, and gas to generate electricity, run vehicles, and power manufacturing and industry.
- Deforestation for agriculture, housing, manufacturing, and other human activities. Deforestation often involves burning, which releases massive amounts of stored carbon back into the atmosphere. This carbon release is compounded by the fact that the area is losing plants, which would take up CO_2 if they were still there.[58] Additionally, bare ground (exposed dirt) also releases carbon back into the atmosphere.[59]
- Conventional agricultural practices, such as tilling (which releases carbon stored in the soil into the atmosphere when it combines with oxygen, forming CO_2), chemical applications, confined animal feeding operations (CAFO), and the use of nitrogen fertilizers.
- Fluorocarbon usage and leaks from equipment such as air conditioners, refrigerators, and heat pumps. Even though these gases are emitted in small quantities, they are generally many thousands of times more efficient than CO_2 at trapping heat (hence, their use in hot-/cold-trapping applications).

Figure 12 is an illustration of the archetype known as *tragedy of the commons*, in which self-interested individual actions exhaust or spoil a common resource. In the case of GHGs, there is no single person or entity at fault since multiple parties are all partaking in the same depletive and destructive actions.

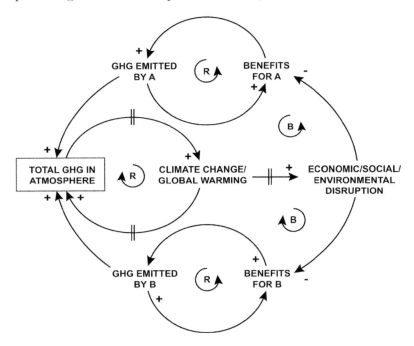

Figure 12: Causal Loop Diagram of Tragedy-of-the-Commons Archetype (GHGs and Climate Change)

As you can see, in this diagram, entities *A* (at top) and *B* (at bottom) benefit from burning fossil fuels, which increases *GHG emitted*. A and B can be individuals or organizations, and they benefit by things like having gas to fuel a car or using energy to cool their computer servers. The more *benefits* A and B receive, the more fossil fuels they tend to burn and *GHG emitted* increases. For example, the more a company with an enormous room full of computer servers profits and grows, the more computers they need, and the more cooling power they need. This results in more economic growth, more business activity, and more demand for computer servers, and so on and so forth. This results in a reinforcing loop that will keep growing until an outside factor stops it.

We also see that as A and B emit greenhouse gases, the *total GHG in atmosphere* (at left) increases. When GHGs increase, after a delayed period (indicated by the double slash), they produce the effect of *climate change/global warming* (center). Climate change, after more delays, causes more greenhouse gases to be released, increasing the *total GHG in the atmosphere* and forming a reinforcing loop.

Climate change also (after delays) creates various types of *economic/social/environmental disruption*, which then reduces the *benefits* that A and B experience. These disruptions come in the form of droughts, fires, floods, biodiversity loss, social unrest, wars, market crashes, global warming, and more—all of which hinder the trade and growth that our economic system requires to function properly. These occurrences form a balancing loop that eventually (after yet another delay) pushes back against GHG emissions.

Now imagine how many more letters we'd need in the alphabet to represent the number of individual cycles in progress and the contribution they make to the GHG/climate change cycle. And even for those who contribute little to GHG production, the climate change effects are felt because they are global in nature.

The major lag between emitting greenhouse gases and the resultant global warming poses a significant problem within the capitalist system. We put GHGs into the atmosphere today, but it can take decades to see the impacts. The mechanisms by which these effects occur are invisible to the human eye, and the lack of visual feedback makes it difficult to convince people to take actions that can often seem to be against their initial best interests, such as spending extra money to install sustainable long-term energy systems. If we don't see immediate feedback or feel an immediate impact from putting GHGs into the atmosphere, we are unlikely to change our behavior. We know without a doubt that GHG emissions from fossil fuels are the cause of the problem at hand, but capitalism provides little incentive to take the action needed to solve it.

Unfortunately, as time goes on, the very nature of the slow-motion climate catastrophe we are trying to prevent will make it more difficult to overcome. It is likely to look like a series of disasters over the coming years and decades in which our society is beaten down, again and again, and recovers a little bit less from each additional blow. If current trends continue, the number of people displaced by natural disasters, floods, wild-fires, crop failures, droughts, and the like will increase dramati-cally. Climate migrants and refugees, such as those from Syria, will be forced to leave areas that are no longer habitable and will go to areas that have more resources—but that may lack *enough* resources to provide for sudden influxes of entire popula-tions. To say that we are woefully unprepared for this future is a vast understatement.

Additionally, it should not be overlooked that it is developed countries who are generating most of the GHG pollution, while it is the less developed countries who feel the impact most imme-diately. So the inequality we discussed earlier is only magnified by this form of resource overshoot.

Let us now look at one more long-term effect of deforesta-tion, desertification, pollution, and anthropogenic climate change: biodiversity loss.

BIODIVERSITY LOSS

Biodiversity loss is a term for the reduction in the overall diversity of plant and animal life on our planet. Since 1970, of 21,000 monitored animal species around the globe, average populations have declined nearly 70 percent. Species in the Caribbean and Latin America have taken the biggest hit, with a 94 percent decline. And global freshwater habitats have lost 84 percent of their populations on average.[60]

This staggering loss is not just sad—it is also a real problem. Human-made systems work with nature at every turn to produce and deliver all the things we take for granted in our lives. We count on nature to cooperate with us and be dependable. When our environment is unpredictable and changes at a faster pace than we can adapt to, the economic systems that rely on those environmental factors are bound to fail. We are starting to see that in supply chain disruptions now. Much blame has been placed on COVID-19 for shipping delays and manufacturing shutdowns, but these supply chain disruptions are also arising because many products are simply not able to be grown, harvested, manufactured, shipped, or otherwise processed because of unpredictable and difficult-to-solve issues with the climate and environment. That coffee you like? We just lost that crop.[61] Those computer chips for those cars? Sorry, but one factory caught fire, the ones in Texas froze, and another in Taiwan is experiencing a drought.[62] Want rice? We're out because there's a drought in California.[63] You might not be able to leave town for a while either, because the only road out just got washed away in a storm, and it will take weeks, maybe even months, to fix.[64]

Weather patterns are changing faster than plants and animals can adapt, and entire ecosystems are being thrown into turmoil. For example, certain species of birds' chicks are no longer hatching to coincide with the lifetime of the caterpillars they rely on for food.[65] Extreme weather events are causing mass die-offs, such as the estimated *billion* sea animals (including starfish, clams, and crabs) that were baked alive in the 2021 Pacific Northwest coastal heat waves.[66] Warming oceans and acidification from excess CO_2 have already killed half the planet's coral reefs.[67] Countless species are having to migrate to higher, cooler climates in what scientists call the "escalator to extinction."

When species go extinct, not only are we losing life forms that will never return to our planet, but we are also losing the very components of the ecosystems upon which we all depend. Whether we like it or not, whether we realize it or not, we are a global, connected community, and we depend upon one another for our collective survival. When major dominos in our ecosystems start to fall due to global warming, changing weather patterns, food-chain disruptions, and natural disasters, we can be certain that there will be ramifications to us as a species.

Whether it be a plant, animal, or insect, the loss of a species has the potential to send consequences cascading throughout the environment, triggering even more untold effects and feedback loops. At this point, the only things we can be 100 percent certain of are that the way of life that most of us are used to is nowhere near sustainable, that because of our negligence our planet and environment will never be the same, and that the more biodiversity we lose, the more unpredictable and difficult our survival as a species will become. Is that not enough to convince us to change our ways?

ARE YOU CONVINCED?

The evidence is clear, and the choice is simple—change course or eventually the very market- and trade-based system that we hold so dear will kill everything we know and love.

But wait. Can't we just tweak the system to make it sustainable? What if we put "guardrails" on capitalism by having better regulations, reining in excessive profits and salaries, redistributing resources and wealth, and adjusting tax policy so rates are more progressive and tax loopholes are eliminated? Won't that solve the problem? No. I'm afraid not, for a number of reasons.

1. Regulations aren't enough. Indeed, "guardrails" appear to be a good starting place in theory. But historically, policy reform and new legislation have been fixes that fail, things that merely treat symptoms and sometimes exacerbate the issues being addressed. The less effective leverage points they use fail to produce the systemic overhaul necessary to create a truly sustainable economy and society.

2. Due to competition, corporations will always keep growing. Until the competition in the market system stops and true collaboration ensues, corporations will only continue to grow and compete for market share, ultimately leaving mass inequality and environmental catastrophe in their wake.

3. Capitalism requires constant activity. Today, practically anything we need or do requires an activity or transaction to take place in which something is monetized. Be it a commodity, labor, or a software program, every transaction uses resources—and the constant, indiscriminate use of resources is one of our main problems. It is an inextricable feature of capitalism and is unsustainable.

4. Capitalism incentivizes exploitation of resources. If you are a capitalist, it is in your best interest to produce and sell as many of something as you can to maximize revenue and profits. That means you are directly incentivized to exploit resources for your own personal gain. Furthermore, as we illustrated in a causal loop diagram in Chapter 3, this incentive runs in direct conflict with the principles of sustainability. Capitalism incentivizes people to produce and sell as many of something as possible. Sustainable practices entail the opposite.

If we want to have a reasonable chance at regenerating our environment and reversing our catastrophic course, we have no choice but to leave behind the systems and tools that have caused these problems in the first place and that continue to perpetuate them. All these consequences—both human and environmental—are caused by, incentivized by, or reinforced by our market system and the pursuit of profit.

Fortunately, we already have the systems and technology to create real, lasting abundance and sustainability. And we are already familiar with what making the transition will take. The trickiest part is putting it all together in a physical form and creating an alternative that obsoletes money and trade.

And that presents us with a choice: do we cling to our old ways, or do we embrace the opportunity to create abundance for all?

We cannot have both. We cannot continue down the road of unchecked growth and selfishness while trying to build a world that respects the limits of nature, the interconnectedness of everything in our environment, and the dignity of all life. We either work together to build a better way of life and make the monetary system obsolete in its entirety, with everything that process entails, or we destroy ourselves and our planet—all for the sake of profit.

In the next part of the book, we look at possible solutions and—if we're brave enough—what a reconstituted world could look like.

PART TWO

THE SOLUTION

The future is already here—it's just not very evenly distributed.

WILLIAM GIBSON

CHAPTER 5

FRAMEWORK FOR A NEW SOCIETY

*All life is interrelated, and we are all caught in an inescapable
network of mutuality, tied in a single garment of destiny.
Whatever affects one directly, affects all indirectly. . . . I can
never be what I ought to be until you are what you ought to be.
And you can never be what you ought to be until I am what I
ought to be—this is the inter-related structure of reality.*

MARTIN LUTHER KING JR.

Most people seem to naturally understand that pieces of paper (or 1s and 0s on a hard drive) aren't worth much in and of themselves. Since they have little intrinsic value, for them to be "worth" something, we must assign value to them. And yet that intellectual understanding doesn't stop many of us from believing that money is a goal in and of itself, to the point that we often fail to recognize it's not really money we're after. Rather, it is what money *provides* that gives us satisfaction. Money grants us access to everything from basic needs to extravagant luxuries. (And it doesn't grant us access to some of the most important things at all.)

This misconception about what we need and desire applies not just to money, but also to the concept of "ownership." We view things as "ours" when we "own" them and therefore can use them whenever we want. But is that the complete story? We might think we want a nice new car, but do we want a car sitting in a garage with a piece of paper that says we "own" it? That's probably not why most people want a new car. More likely we want access to a car (maybe a *nice* car) when we need it, and we want that car to get us from point A to point B. While the car's looks or status might come into play to a degree, most of us probably want the *transportation* more than anything. If we all had access to autonomous vehicles that picked us up and dropped us off for free whenever and wherever we needed it, I suspect most of us wouldn't care if they lacked the ability to go from zero to one hundred in 2.3 seconds flat, as long as they were clean, comfortable, and reliable. Likewise, rather than wanting to "own" a nice house (aside from the financial and economic "benefits" that come from owning a house within the capitalist system), what most of us likely want is a *home* we can call our own—one that provides us with comfort, security, privacy, and space to conduct our daily activities and relax.

This misplaced desire for ownership goes deeper than we might think. Our marketing-driven, consumerist society fixates on buying and "owning" so many things that we don't even realize what we are missing, because we are too busy earning, spending, and consuming. As Charles Eisenstein says in *The More Beautiful World Our Hearts Know Is Possible,*[68]

> The objects of our selfish desires are but substitutes for what we really want. Advertisers play on this all the time, selling sports cars as a substitute for freedom, junk food and soda as a substitute for excitement, "brands" as a substitute for social identity, and pretty much everything as a substitute for sex, itself a proxy for the intimacy that

is so lacking in modern life. We might also see sports hero worship as a substitute for the expression of one's own greatness, amusement parks as a substitute for the transcending of boundaries, pornography as a substitute for self-love, and overeating as a substitute for connection or the feeling of being present. What we really need is nearly unavailable in the lives that society offers us.

Think about the difference between *owning* and *experiencing*. Do you experience everything you own? Maybe. Maybe not. Have you ever bought a book you didn't read? Or a piece of exercise equipment you've hardly used? Do you need to own something to experience it? Clearly not. You don't have to own a car to drive it. You don't have to own a house to live in it.

Books and exercise equipment are perfect examples of things that are already commonly shared by many people in modern society at libraries and gyms. That raises the question: What if we could experience the things we want without ownership? What if things like transportation, food, energy; a home and community; opportunities to contribute, learn, grow, and experience our potential; security and comfort . . . what if all those things could be available *without* money? The answer: They can be—if we choose to make them so. If we can create the experiences that money currently provides, minus the paywalls, the need and desire for money would be eliminated and *money would become obsolete*.

The trick is to create the systems and structures that would *allow* money to become obsolete. However, how do we build these new systems? What philosophy should these new systems and structures be based upon? If our current system is based on competition, and we need to curtail the effects of competition, then it would make sense to adopt principles of cooperation instead. But can humans really cooperate effectively enough to come up with a system that can make money obsolete? Let us see what Charles Darwin, the "father of evolution," might think about that question . . .

FROM COMPETITION TO COOPERATION

When Darwin used the phrase "survival of the fittest," he was referring not to strength or physical fitness, but to the idea that members of a species who have characteristics best suited to a particular environment are more likely to survive and reproduce, thus reinforcing those characteristics over time. In their book *Survival of the Friendliest*,[69] Brian Hare of Duke University's Center for Cognitive Neuroscience and award-winning journalist Vanessa Woods posit that in most cases, qualities like friendliness, communication, and cooperation determine the longevity of a species.

Cooperative relationships can be seen throughout nature. Colonies of ants (which estimates show make up 15 to 25 percent of all animal biomass on earth[70]) are known for their cooperative behaviors. Flowers and bees have mutually beneficial relationships that have proven successful for millions of years. The friendliest wolves adapted their behavior—and eventually their appearance and genetic makeup—to become "man's best friend." In 2020, roughly 15,000 wolves lived in the United States, two-thirds of them in Alaska.[71] How many dogs are there in the US? Roughly 90 million.[72]

Emma M. Seppälä, PhD, science director for the Center for Compassion and Altruism Research and Education at Stanford University elaborates:

It is not surprising that compassion is a natural tendency since it is essential for human survival. As has been brought to light by Keltner, the term "survival of the fittest," often attributed to Charles Darwin, was actually coined by Herbert Spencer and Social Darwinists who wished to justify class and race superiority. A lesser known fact is that Darwin's work is best described with the phrase "survival of the kindest." Indeed, in *The Descent of Man* and *Selection in Relation to Sex*, Darwin argued for "the greater strength of the social or maternal instincts than that of any other instinct or motive." In another passage, he comments that "communities, which included the greatest number of the most sympathetic members, would flourish best, and rear the greatest number of off-spring." Compassion may indeed be a naturally evolved and adaptive trait. Without it, the survival and flourishing of our species would have been unlikely.[73]

Unfortunately, the monetary system has stripped our society of two of its most important core elements—cooperation and empathy. In our pursuit of profit and ownership, many of us have forgotten what it feels like to work together to contribute to the well-being of the people around us, to know that we are part of a community that is interdependent for survival and that provides the psychologically nourishing bonds of camaraderie and love. Many have also forgotten what it is like to be a steward of the earth—observing it, caring for it, helping it re-generate and heal from errors of the past. Many fail to see that we are all part of a global ecosystem and that it is impossible to do anything without affecting us all on some level.

Without recognizing that the world and people around us are an extension of ourselves, we'll remain in search of a substitute for that missing connection to fulfillment and belonging. To survive as a species, we must return to being "friendly" with each other and the earth, as will be apparent in the principles that underpin our new systems.

PRINCIPLES OF A MONEYLESS SOCIETY

While we must end the current systems that incentivize exploitation of labor and resources in exchange for profit, we cannot simply abolish money or profit outright. Snapping our fingers—poof!—and calling them "illegal" would not solve the problems we currently face and would only exacerbate many already-dire situations. The goal instead is to develop new systems that people naturally turn toward to gain a healthier, more sustainable, and more attractive way of life; money becomes obsolete only as a result.

To this end, we must intentionally cooperate to create innovative new communities that position us for long-term environmental and social stability in a setting where money is not required to produce everyday goods or necessities. This can be done by creating what is often called a *post-scarcity society* or *post-scarcity economy*, in which there is no longer a need for money or profit because necessities (and "luxuries") are abundant and provided to everyone for free through automation and environmentally friendly regenerative systems and technologies. Myriad systems, structures, tools, processes, and technologies that could help us transition to a world without money already exist. Many of these developments, though, are still fragmented and not capable of being utilized to their full potential within the capitalist system; nor are they combined or used in a manner that would assist in a transition to a moneyless society.

To reach the goal of obsoleting money and trade, we must consciously choose guiding principles and then engineer them to coordinate in ways that produce abundance, equity, and freedom from the need for money or trade. The rest of this chapter describes foundational principles that, together, can construct the workings of an equitable, sustainable moneyless society. Then, in the following chapter, we'll look at what these principles might look like in action, as well as some innovative systems, organizations, people, and technologies already leading us into this future.

HIGHEST GOOD OF ALL

Our first and overarching principle is the concept of the "highest good of all." This encompasses the idea of acting in a manner that is in the best interest of everyone, not just ourselves or a small, select group. This common-sense approach advocates empathy, communication, transparency, and working through our differences to create positive transformation for all life on Earth, with the overarching theme of stewardship for one another and our environment.

Acting for the highest good of all is the core, foundational principle upon which all the other principles of a moneyless society are based, and it applies in terms of proactively addressing our problems in a manner that considers our biosphere, its present populations, and its future generations (future generations in particular with respect to climate change). The focus shifts from "What can I get for myself?" to "What works best for everyone now and in the future?" Another way of phrasing this principle might be "If it doesn't work for everybody, it doesn't work for anybody."

Of all the principles on the list, this one is likely the most challenging to achieve. Of course, in most situations we can never actually get to a perfect solution for everyone, but we can maximize results and work with good intent toward that end. Yes, it will take a great deal of effort; however, this is the challenge of our times—to figure out solutions that work for and can be supported by everyone involved. We must strive for this ideal to achieve the best results possible for all people and all life, everywhere on the planet.

COOPERATIVE/SHARING ECONOMY

Next up is a cooperative/sharing economy. While I am combining the ideas of cooperation and sharing here in this section, I distinguish them as such:

- *Sharing* is multiple people having access to a thing or things.
- *Cooperation* includes the concept of sharing but also encompasses people working together to achieve things that they could not accomplish on their own.

A cooperative/sharing economy is one in which individuals, organizations, and regions work together to share progress, resources, and information; and collaborate to maximize effort and efficiency, reduce redundancy, and create the most universally beneficial results possible. If you think of competition and cooperation as being two ends of a spectrum, our economy is currently skewed so far to the extreme of competition that constant, multiple destructive externalities are inevitable. The principles of cooperation and sharing seek to restore a balance and build a framework that fosters cooperative actions and relationships in our society and economy.

In a cooperative/sharing economic structure, competition is not eliminated or forbidden; we simply recognize that in many situations, cooperation and collaboration produce superior results with less effort, less redundancy, and fewer resources. But competition in the overall economy, in the labor market as well as in the public sector and many aspects of daily life, will for the most part become obsolete and be replaced with systems for giving everyone, regardless of their contribution, free and unlimited access to all necessities, as well as access to many other goods and services as they are needed.

Cooperation and sharing on a local level will mean, for example, people working together to develop localized, automated systems for no-cost food, water, and energy production for everyone in the community. On a national or international level, it will mean that instead of countries competing with one another, they share resources and raw materials for the benefit of all, as well as innovations and information that can help reduce unnecessary redundancies and conserve resources. Instead of continuing to extract resources for profit from already-depleted areas, regions will pool assets to invest in the regeneration of ecologically debilitated areas of the planet, thereby also investing in local people and communities. These collaborative international actions directly and simultaneously fight both climate change and inequality.

Within the idea of a cooperative/sharing economy are two critical concepts: open-source information and universal basic goods and services.

Open-Source Information. To facilitate a cooperative or sharing economy, information must be more freely available. That is, it must be *open-source information.* Documents and records that don't expose individual, private, or sensitive information will be open for inspection by the general public. Information concerning production processes, designs, formulas, and other information that is currently copyrighted or kept proprietary to private companies (but could be of public benefit) will be available for any individual or entity to use, examine, build upon, and distribute. These systems will inherently encourage high levels of collaboration, public accountability, and transparency in matters regarding public goods production or societal and economic design and decision-making.

Universal Basic Goods & Services. A critical system for moving to a moneyless society is a system often called *universal basic goods and services (UBGS)*. This concept means that everyone in a community or society receives everything they need to operate, survive, and thrive within that society. Everyone, regardless of their contribution, receives free food, housing, clothing, household goods, electricity, computers, internet access, and whatever else is needed to go about day-to-day life.

Many goods and services will come to us via different systems and infrastructure than presently exist. Resources that now sit idle for a significant amount of time, such as cars, will be available via an access-based system to maximize their usefulness. There will also be a focus on providing access to larger non-consumables that many people currently might not have access to, such as recreational vehicles, physical fitness equipment, art and music supplies, or technology like 3D printers. In essence, the concept of "ownership" will become obsolete in many situations, since having unobstructed access to practically all needs and many additional wants will eliminate the false pretense that one must own property to survive or thrive.

This concept is similar to but fundamentally different from the concept of *universal basic income (UBI)*, in which people receive money instead of the actual goods and products that are needed. The concept of universal basic goods and services is a fundamental component of the systems that integrate to form a moneyless society. We will discuss the initial transition to and development of such a system via a network of cooperatives in Chapter 7.

SOCIAL JUSTICE

Social justice is the fair treatment of everyone, including those who have been marginalized or discriminated against in the past. Social justice entails the principle of investing in others, especially those who need the most. It involves investing in communities, in the land, in nature, in the world around us, without any expectation of personal reciprocation. We do it because we know that the world will be better off because of it. If the concept of profit had an opposite, social justice would likely be it. As we discussed in the first part of this book, profit creates competition, and competition in a market society leads to inequality, poverty, structural violence, and many other devastating externalities. The ultimate in social justice would be doing away with the profit motive and returning the resources and means of production from private corporations and investors to the people, so that the farms, machines, factories, resources, institutions, and opportunities can benefit everyone and the planet alike.

To clarify what we mean by social justice, let's look at definitions for inequality, equality, equity, and justice, four highly related terms that are often conflated.

- *Inequality*: When people have unequal access to resources or opportunities.
- *Equality*: Distributing opportunities and resources evenly, regardless of preexisting circumstances of inequality.
- *Equity*: Distributing resources or opportunities in a manner that identifies and addresses existing inequalities, so that a more equal outcome is realized.

- *Justice*: Restructuring or fixing the system that produced the inequalities, so that everyone has equal access to future resources and opportunities.

In Figure 13, we see a drawing of a heavily laden apple tree leaning toward the left.

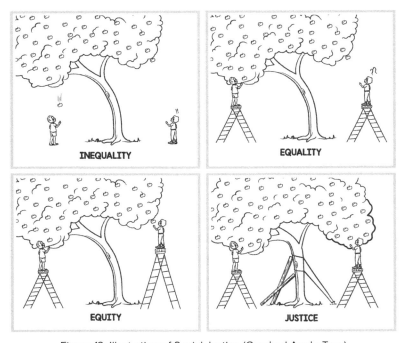

Figure 13: Illustration of Social Justice (Crooked Apple Tree)

Inequality is represented by the person on the left catching more fruit than the person on the right because most of the fruit is on that side. By providing each person with the same size stepladder, we have provided *equality*. However, since the tree is still leaning, the ladder helps the person on the left reach the fruit on the tree, but for the person on the right the ladder is not tall enough to do the same, demonstrating that an equal solution often does not produce an equal outcome for those with initial disadvantages. *Equity* attempts to address these disadvantages—in this case by providing the person on the right a taller ladder so both people can now reach the fruit. However, *justice* has not been achieved until the imbalances in the systems have been corrected—that is, until the tree itself has been straightened, providing every person with access, regardless of their position around the tree.

As an example outside of crooked apple trees, if we were to give laptop computers to children for distance learning in an *equal* manner, every child would get a laptop, regardless of whether they already had one—so some of the laptops distributed would likely not be used, which would mean wasted resources. Not only that, but by attempting to distribute a laptop to every child, the supply of laptops would be more likely to run out before every child received one. If we were to distribute laptops in a more *equitable* manner, we would first give them to students who did not have a laptop. If we were to exercise *social justice* in this situation, we would focus on correcting the systemic problems that cause the laptops to be distributed in an unequal manner to begin with.

The principle of social justice goes beyond the concept of equity in many ways. Instead of simply making up for a lack in the present, social justice seeks to undo and reconcile hundreds of years of oppression and continued inequality in marginalized populations, such as Blacks, Hispanics/Latinos, and Indigenous peoples. It is fundamentally against the nature of our competitive market economy to resolve any of the inequalities that continue to be perpetuated in modern society. By making focused and intentional investments (both monetary and otherwise) in these marginalized or disadvantaged communities, institutions, and environments, we can systematically restructure our world and way of life to create equal access and opportunities—in a new type of society—for everyone. When social justice is realized in this fashion, each person has the chance to fulfill their true potential and the opportunity to grow, learn, contribute, and thrive.

It should be noted that this application of social justice applies not only to race and ethnicity but to any qualities that have engendered discrimination and systemic bias: sex, gender, sexual preference, religion, class, and so on. The social justice principle builds on progress from many movements, including women's rights, civil rights, LGBTQ+ rights, Black Lives Matter, and others.

After several generations of significant investments in social justice throughout society (and in combination with the other systems and principles in this section), the disparity between the least and the most privileged will largely vanish. Our mass inequality will be replaced by an unparalleled system with an abundance of necessities, equal rights, equitable freedoms, and opportunities, as well as an absence of the systemic oppression or structural violence currently inherent in the market economy.

ECOLOGICAL BALANCE

Ecological balance is a broad principle that encompasses the myriad relationships between our environment, the biosphere, and our socioeconomic system. It involves the sustainable management and regeneration of resources, along with other interactions with and investments in our biosphere. In essence, this principle is the art of consuming *less* while investing in our environment *more*. It is about discovering all the creative ways we can regenerate our planet using innovative, sustainable technologies.

The principle of ecological balance encapsulates concepts such as:

- *Post Growth/Degrowth*: A phase or era of controlled economic contraction, enabling us to curtail much of the unnecessary activity generated by the capitalist market system, thereby more effectively addressing resource overshoot and climate change.
- *Circular Economy/Closed-Loop Economy*: An economic system by which all "waste" outputs are utilized as inputs for other purposes. Recycling, reusing, upgrading, upcycling, repurposing, and retrofitting are all techniques used in this category.
- *Agroecology and Regenerative Agriculture*: Agroecology is an approach to agriculture that takes into account the entire ecosystem and impacts on it. Regenerative agriculture is a subset of agroecology focused on restoring the health of the soil and environment.

Without the need for competition and growth, private interests will not be driven to exploit and pollute our planet as they are now, and the endless activity and fossil fuel consumption required to sustain the capitalist system will largely be eliminated. Much of the population will no longer need to commute to a job, and for the travel that is needed, most forms of transportation will be automated, free, and powered by renewable energy. By localizing or regionalizing the production of goods and resources whenever possible, the distance items must travel will be minimized and overseas shipping will be reduced to a small percentage of the current amount. In addition to reducing fossil fuel consumption, we will also likely reduce the non-compostable, single-use plastic industry to a single-digit percentage of its current size.

The principle of ecological balance works in conjunction with other principles on our list to effectively manage limited quantities of resources and produce more sustainable results.

For instance, many social justice practices would be geared toward regenerative agriculture to sustainably create an abundance of food for previously underserved populations, while also using the principles of technology and a sharing economy. This approach enables us to simultaneously regenerate our environment, address social issues, and provide ourselves with what we need.

ABUNDANCE THROUGH SCIENCE & TECHNOLOGY

Implementing science and technology to the greatest extent possible will be a key component in the functioning of an effective and efficient moneyless society. Currently, conflicting interests resulting from the profit motive keep many of the most effective applications of technical progress at bay. This principle effectively gives the systems of production and automation a new purpose—that of creating abundance for humanity rather than profits for companies.

In repurposing our technology, we are utilizing one of the most effective leverage points possible, and the results will be profound. Without conflicting monetary interests, we can more fully utilize and implement the most current findings to make educated decisions regarding building effective systems. Rigorous research and experimentation, decoupled from the monetary system, will help us cultivate and refine more effective methods for progress, efficiency, and sustainability.

When free from private ownership and properly applied to production and distribution systems, automation will eliminate large portions of unnecessary or dangerous labor and will help provide numerous goods and services at no monetary cost. Automation is here whether we like it or not—in the business world, in production, distribution, information, energy, medicine, in our homes. We would do well to embrace it in a democratic, equitable manner and not let private interests dictate what our automated future looks like.

Entire swaths of jobs, functions, and roles in society could be automated, eliminated, powered by renewable energy, or made much more sustainable. Positions and functions such as food delivery, trucking, grocery stores, coffee shops, clothing stores, car dealerships, and auto repair would be restructured entirely, obsoleted, or automated. Furthermore, many jobs people hold today are what the late author and anthropologist David Graeber called "bullshit jobs"[74]—jobs of little to no consequence or importance to humanity as a whole. These positions often just keep people busy, giving them a paycheck for providing redundant or unnecessary services or products. Many of these jobs, including practically anything having to do with the financial sector, do little more than support the functioning of the competitive monetary system. They could be eliminated right now and the only thing anybody would care about is the profits missed or jobs lost—not the actual work performed.

With the application of technology and automation under socially just, ecologically balanced systems, we will have access to nutritious food, comfortable homes, safe water, renewable energy, a good education system, and community resources—and we will flourish.

LIBERTY & FREEDOM

Liberty and freedom encompass the ability to freely choose for yourself what path to take in life, where to live, what to study, and when and how to contribute your time and labor to society. While there may be a nuance in definition (*liberty* having a more internal sense, such as being able to choose how to think or what to believe; and *freedom* having a more external sense, such as not being imprisoned), the two terms are often used interchangeably and are generally accepted as the unrestricted access and capability to do what one pleases, as long as one's actions do not bring harm to another.

In a moneyless society, individuals, organizations, and regions will enjoy the freedom to act autonomously. Anyone can travel, work, play, and worship in any manner they please, to the reasonable extent that it does not harm other individuals or sensitive environments or species. (To clarify, I advocate that there should be acceptable limits for things like the quantity of resources one can use or destroy without the consent of others.)

Furthermore, all contribution and labor will be voluntary, not enforced by any means, or by any person or entity; likewise with the choice of what labor, contribution, or field of study any individual wishes to pursue. As today, there will be labor needed within a vast spectrum of tasks and duties. Working conditions and locations will certainly vary, and there may be benefits or privileges that come with specific skillsets or a higher level of education, but the possibilities for contribution are endless. A person might volunteer to help install a solar farm in Bali, then volunteer to help with an automated garden project in Africa, then decide to go back to school in the northeast US.

This tends to be a difficult concept for a lot of people to wrap their head around—that there won't be any force or coercion necessary to induce people to work and contribute to society. We will discuss this objection and the process of transitioning to a volunteer labor system in greater detail in upcoming chapters. However, let us say this for now: this is the same system of freedoms and liberties that we enjoy currently in the United States (once we are of age to act as an adult)—the freedom to choose our own life path without being told or forced by the government or any other person or entity to do or work at anything. There is no loss of freedom. By adding the other principles into the equation, by creating abundance and a cooperative economy, we no longer must sell our labor in exchange for money to survive, and we experience *greater* freedom.

ANTIFRAGILITY

Antifragility is the act of something growing stronger in the face of shock or adversity. The concept was developed by Nassim Nicholas Taleb in his 2012 book, *Antifragile: Things That Gain from Disorder*.[75] This concept goes beyond resilience to a point that a system will not only be capable of resisting shock but will be improved upon when confronted with near-failure or breakdown. If a society is antifragile, it not only resiliently navigates crisis situations but also reassesses and improves whenever presented with the opportunity. In essence, it is the socio-economic manifestation of the strongest leverage point: the ability to let go of or adopt paradigms and perspectives with little difficulty or resistance. It is a fluid, dynamic, ever-evolving state of seeking, understanding, adjusting, decision-making, and collaboration.

Our current system is fragile—it is the opposite of anti-fragile. With profits being at the center of our system, anything that jeopardizes the realization of profits threatens the stability of the entire system. For a perfect example of how *not* to be antifragile, look at what happened with the economy during COVID-19. Our economic system practically broke down because the endless activity required by capitalism was forced to come to a grinding halt in many regions of the world nearly simultaneously. If we had been economically antifragile, not only would we have been able to handle the COVID-19 epidemic effectively and efficiently, but we also would have stepped back and used the situation to gain an objective awareness of exactly where our medical and pandemic-response systems were lacking and could be improved, thereby making the systems more resilient the next time such a situation should occur.

This principle includes both economic and ecological antifragility. In *ecological* antifragility, our relationship to and stewardship of our ecological environment improves with each instance of shock and variability. A perfect example of this is climate change. We can move toward ecological antifragility in this instance by employing methodologies like regenerative agriculture and holistic grazing practices to restore soil health and sequester carbon from the atmosphere. We can build *economic* antifragility by using a degrowth strategy to assist in our ecological goals. This would enable us to reduce production amounts and energy use in many sectors, while simultaneously using sharing principles to improve distribution and utilization.

As with anything, trial and error are necessary and will be inevitable. Corrections will always have to be made along the way. Assess, adjust, and reassess. Society can't make a change overnight; it must evolve and make its evolution a conscious process. Progress and development are constant exercises in noticing patterns of what works best and applying what we learn from our mistakes and failures. No one has all the answers, and we must learn and grow together. If we can do that as a society, then we have a chance at building the systems of the future, today.

CREATING SYNERGY

While each of these principles already exists in our modern society, at least in certain circumstances, it is the combination of them and the way they work together synergistically to form a cohesive society that can provide an abundance of goods and services, while simultaneously increasing the quality of life and eliminating the need for endless unnecessary activity.

In the next chapter, we will begin to look at some specific systems and structures and how they can operate together to form a more robust foundation upon which we can build a new socially just, sustainable economy and society.

CHAPTER 6

FUTURE SYSTEMS
IN ACTION

*Think of it. We are blessed with technology that would be
indescribable to our forefathers. We have the wherewithal,
the know-it-all to feed everybody, clothe everybody, and give every
human on Earth a chance. We know now what we could never
have known before—that we now have the option for all
humanity to 'make it' successfully on this planet in this lifetime.
Whether it is to be Utopia or Oblivion will be a touch-and-go
relay race right up to the final moment.*

R. BUCKMINSTER FULLER, ARCHITECT, INVENTOR, AUTHOR,
SYSTEMS THEORIST, AND FUTURIST

I have often heard people cynically call the type of society described in this book a utopia—"a place of ideal perfection especially in laws, government, and social conditions"[76]—a place that, as the name suggests (Greek prefix *ou*, meaning "not," and *topos*, meaning "place"), does not exist.

Is a moneyless society "ideal perfection"? No, it is not. Not even close.

A better word for the society we speak of is a *protopia*, or a society that moves in a positive direction by functioning with balance and synergy. This idea stands in stark contrast to today's society, which is barreling toward the *dystopian* end of the spectrum. The protopian society we speak of is not perfect, but it is a society that operates in an overall positive fashion, and it keeps evolving and getting better over time. Rather than dreaming about some unobtainable state of utopia, striving to create a protopia is much more realistic.

Furthermore, please bear in mind that just as there is a difference between a utopia and a protopia, a large difference also exists between the evolved society we speak of—as in what a moneyless society might eventually look like—and the transitional period that it will take to build that society. While we may call the communities that begin to model this framework a "moneyless society" or a "protopian civilization," implementing the level of integration, infrastructure, and automation described in this book will likely take several generations of restructuring our social and economic systems. We'll discuss the transitional process in the next chapter.

In this chapter, my main goal is to illustrate how the principles described in the last chapter work in synergy to create new social and economic systems, and to present you with an idea of how the elimination of the profit motive affects the operation and integrity of the systems overall. We are not going to get into detail about all the individual systems and how they will operate, because methods will differ from place to place, depending on a variety of factors. Plus, many technologies created in the coming decades, while new types of communities are in formation, will be more evolved than what is available at the time of this writing and will no doubt render many details obsolete. But hold onto your hats, because first we're going to look at the most complicated systems diagram in this book: an overview of a potential moneyless society.

PICTURE OF A MONEYLESS SOCIETY

Figure 14 (next page) maps out some of the potential relationships between the elements that could form the structure of a moneyless society (sans plus and minus signs) and illustrates the degree of interconnectedness between them.

The diagram includes two primary goals in boxes: *universal basic goods and services* and *social, ecological, and economic prosperity*. Principles, systems, and other elements in the giant diagram include: *highest good of all*; *public accountability*; *transparency*; *open-source systems*; *feedback systems and public decision-making tools*; *equality, equity, and social justice*; *sharing economy*; *ecological balance*; *agroecology and regenerative agriculture*; *natural and technological abundance*; *localization*; *modularization*; *automation*; *efficient production*; *innovation*; *elimination of unnecessary labor*; *cooperation*; *contribution and volunteerism*; and *community development and investment*.

Instead of my explaining every relationship in this diagram, I invite you to ponder the relationships between the elements and to think about how and why some of these relationships exist. Without worrying about the plus or minus signs (as far as I have been able to discern, they would all be pluses in this diagram, as it seems that everything would contribute to everything else positively in this scenario), what are some of the reinforcing loops you notice? In what ways do the principles listed in the last chapter affect the way all these variables interact with each other? What are some relationships and feedback loops that are not shown with the connecting arrows—for example, how might innovation contribute to equality, equity, and social justice, and vice versa? How can open-source systems contribute to automation technology? How can cooperation contribute to regenerating the environment? How does regenerating the environment contribute to investing in the community?

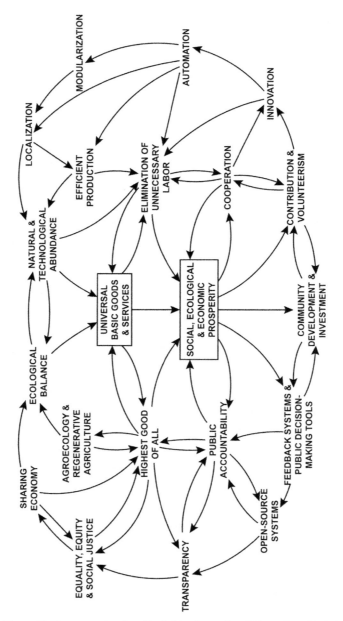

Figure 14: Components of an Equitable, Operational Moneyless Society

Ultimately, all the factors in the diagram interact with each other to achieve the goal of providing members of society with everything needed to function in daily life for free without the need to trade one's time, labor, or money, and all while investing both in people and the environment. This means people get what they need to live and are no longer compelled to generate end-less economic activity just to keep the capitalist system functioning. It also means that the planet gets a break—no longer having to provide us with endless amounts of resources and energy just to keep the wheels turning on a massive trade-based system.

What we have in our current economic system is *trade-based reciprocity*, or *transactional reciprocity*. That means that practically everything we need and use must be procured through trade or transactions. And because everything must be traded, we also need currency, which means we also need jobs and cars and all the other things that come with the transaction-based lives we have created for ourselves.

The diagram of a moneyless society illustrates *systemic reciprocity*. That means that instead of people conducting trans-actions to deliver things from one individual or company to the next, we utilize systems and structures that provide an abun-dance of necessities, while eliminating as much human labor as possible. Because there is no need to pay bills to survive, and because people don't need to work forty hours a week to pay for their necessities, they would have greater amounts of free time that could be spent on activities they *want* to do.

What happens when people get what they need for free—water, food, housing, clothing, household goods, electricity, edu-cation, healthcare, internet access, technology, transportation? What happens when people have what they need to realize their goals and dreams? They prosper, and their communities pros-per. And when people prosper, they are more able and willing to contribute to society. They contribute what they can, when they can, where they can, and the system takes care of everyone in return. That's *systemic reciprocity.*

In complex systems such as a functioning moneyless society, it is impossible to list all the relationship dynamics and the ways they affect one another. The illustration in Figure 14 is simply one rendition of how these principles and relationships can work together to create a sustainable, equitable society. And with as many arrows and relationships as are shown, we could add many more, but the diagram would become unnecessarily difficult to read.

Many of the elements shown are things we've already talked about, and nearly all of them exist in today's world, but they are distorted and weakened significantly by the main factor we have removed from this diagram: profit. Without the element of profit to incentivize hoarding of private property and surplus wealth, there is no creation of vastly unequal outcomes for different groups of people, and no pitting of environmental integrity against business interests. Once the profit element is absent, all the elements of the diagram can complement each other, flowing from one point to the next, each adding its part to form a dynamic, circulating whole.

Notice that when we eliminate profit, we also essentially eliminate the ownership of private property and the ownership of any surplus that property produces. (Remember that the right to *personal* property, as we discussed in Chapter 1, remains intact.) Surplus and the machines, factories, and land that produce it are no longer owned by any one person or private interests but rather are owned and shared collectively by the community or network of communities. This foundational shift in ownership eliminates the success-to-the-successful archetype we saw repeatedly in Chapter 3. In other words, it is the combination of the elements and the purpose driving them that allows us to realize the initial goal of *universal basic goods and services*, which helps realize the greater goal of *social, ecological, and economic balance and prosperity.*

Let's look at a few familiar subsystems and how they function without the profit motive. Since we started with the labor system before as an example that most of us are familiar with and that links to so many other systems, let's look at it first in this context as well.

LABOR & CONTRIBUTION

One of the most common objections to a moneyless society is that people won't want to work—that there will be "too many lazy people" and "nobody will clean the toilets." Labor is the basis for any society, so what will motivate people to work?

The answer is simple. People will be motivated by the same thing that motivates people in a monetary economy, and the same thing that motivated people to work long before money even existed: positive reinforcement. That is, being rewarded with positive feedback when desired behaviors are performed. The only difference in a moneyless society is that positive reinforcement will come from sources other than money—such as a sense of contribution or accomplishment, the development of personal or community relationships, physical benefits from the contributions themselves, personal gifts, favors, or accolades. We receive these types of positive reinforcement today, but the profit motive seems to make them all take a back seat. Without a central focus on money, profit, and material possessions, other aspects of positive reinforcement will simply return to the forefront and guide our systems for rewarding labor.

Figure 15 illustrates the positive reinforcement that comes from shared social, economic, and ecological progress.

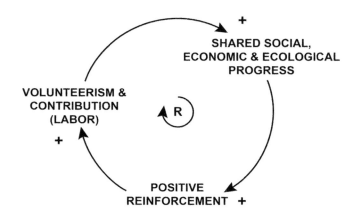

Figure 15: Causal Loop Diagram of Labor Market without Profit

As you can see in this simple clockwise cycle, *volunteerism and contribution (labor)* leads to *shared social, economic, and ecological progress*, which leads to *positive reinforcement*. The positive reinforcement then leads to more volunteer contributions, and the cycle repeats itself in a reinforcing loop. Since profit and the ownership of surplus are absent, and the benefits of labor and surplus are distributed evenly throughout the community, there is no success-to-the-successful dynamic to separate this illustration into the haves and the have-nots.

We can also insert numerous industry-specific elements into this diagram. For example, labor in the healthcare setting might look like Figure 16. After *volunteerism and contribution (labor)*, we have inserted *free, innovative healthcare solutions*, which gives us more detail about the labor performed and its results. We could illustrate labor being performed in multiple other sectors or industries in this manner—energy, agriculture, education, transportation, manufacturing, childcare. The dynamic is the same.

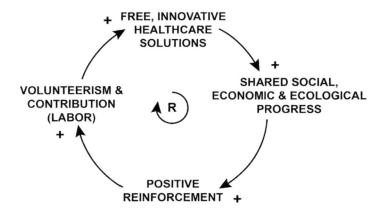

Figure 16: Causal Loop Diagram of Healthcare Labor Market without Profit

Positive reinforcement acts as a catalyst and influential driver across the board, generated in many forms and fashions. If cultivated and utilized properly, it can inspire people to volunteer and contribute their labor throughout society. Conversely, if there is no shared social, economic, or ecological progress, and therefore no subsequent positive reinforcement for a specific labor or task, that task is not as likely to be performed again.

Additionally, as we discussed in Chapter 5, many of today's human-filled jobs will become largely automated. Jobs or roles that do not directly contribute to producing what is needed to operate in modern society or to promoting the well-being of humans or the environment will simply be eliminated: many food-service positions can already be automated, the financial sector will become obsolete, and a significant portion of the legal sector (which to a large degree manages the competitive monetary system) will also be obsolete.

For those who work at scheduled positions, workloads will likely be greatly reduced. "Full-time" work hours may be in the vicinity of three to five hours per day for most duties, with a four-day workweek also being likely. Due to fewer overall tasks needing to be performed by humans, more people will be available when needed. Mutual aid agreements between individuals or communities will also likely be employed in various circumstances.

Closely related to the labor system is the education system. While a discussion of the education system is outside the scope of this book for any number of reasons, I want to make two quick points. First, educational requirements for some jobs will still exist, although there might be more options to meet those requirements—for example, less focus on the "degree" approach and more focus on obtaining and applying relevant skills and knowledge. Second, all levels of education will be free and accessible to everyone, likely through a digital education platform available worldwide that can be navigated individually or used in an instructor-led classroom setting. Ultimately, the better the education system, the better society can function in all its different aspects. The better equipped people become to contribute meaningfully to society, the better society will function, and the more progress will be made.

HOUSING & SUSTAINABLE COMMUNITIES

In our current capitalist society, the housing system is closely linked to the labor/wage system, resulting in a misallocation of housing resources that leaves multiple housing units sitting empty for every homeless person in the US. By removing profit from the equation, we shift our focus from "being able to afford a home" to "creating sustainable communities." According to sustain.org, "A sustainable community manages its human, natural, and financial capital to meet current needs while ensuring that adequate resources are available for future generations."

In achieving this outcome, three key approaches are likely to come into play: retrofitting, automation, and localization.

Retrofitting. There are currently numerous old shopping malls, abandoned industrial facilities, and other structures that can be retrofitted and improved to become free housing and sustainable communities. Unused shopping centers are already being converted into schools and community centers, and into communities for homeless or disadvantaged people. Over time, countless additional buildings will also free up as the jobs they currently house become obsolete, leading to opportunities for refitting those buildings for vertical farms, indoor agriculture, carbon-sequestering technologies, community centers, educational facilities, fitness facilities, art centers, and many other possibilities.

Automation. Large-scale 3D printing and other automated technologies are likely to constitute most housing and facility construction in the future. Smaller 3D-printed neighborhoods are already popping up around the globe. This trend will only accelerate as the technology improves and becomes less expensive. Sustainable replacements for concrete and wood will be needed, however, because the scale of current use of both materials is unsustainable.[77] Many alternatives already exist, and more will be developed and utilized in the future.

Localization. A primary goal for sustainable communities is to maximize local production and minimize transportation and externalities caused by production. The more communities can supply their own food, water, energy, resources, and finished products, the more likely they are to achieve a regenerative, closed-loop economy that is sustainable and carbon-negative. In addition, if numerous communities in a region are self-sustaining, they can network, share, and create mutual aid agreements with each other, which increases resiliency against outside shocks.

WELLNESS (HEALTHCARE & CRIMINAL JUSTICE)

One of the best measures of the overall quality of life in an area or region is the wellness level of the people who live there. Because the structure of a holistically designed moneyless society addresses so many issues in both the healthcare system and the criminal justice system simultaneously, these two systems will likely not be looked upon as isolated aspects of our lives in the future. Many of the crimes, actions, diseases, and outcomes that manifest seemingly out of nowhere today, but that are actually the results of living circumstances, will be addressed through systemic intervention and a restructuring of our socioeconomic system.

Instead of treating symptoms after they arise and working to mitigate the effects of a dysfunctional social and economic system, the first step in a holistic wellness system is prevention via ensuring that people have everything they need to live a happy, healthy life. Investments are made where people are lacking the most—in the environment around them, their homes, their jobs, their families, their communities, food, resources, and so on—to remedy problems at their core and prevent them from happening in the future.

Many of the things that tend to boost a community's well-being—parks, recreational and athletic facilities, job training, schools, libraries, clinics, nutritious food, community centers, resources—also tend to reduce crime. These things will all be free and accessible to anyone in a moneyless society.

Food quality will be addressed in both agriculture and processing. Soil quality will be improved through regenerative agriculture to make sure produce is packed with as many nutrients as possible. Most, if not all, toxins, pesticides, and other harmful chemicals will be eliminated from both agriculture and food production altogether. Less healthy foods will be discouraged through better nutritional education and the absence of constant marketing; more nutritious foods will be encouraged and made widely available through automated, local production methods. Additionally, conflicts of interest in nutritional research will be eliminated, potentially leading to clearer dietary guidelines and a healthier population.

A population that has not been deprived of rest or exercise, that has access to nutritious food, and that has not been induced by clever marketing campaigns to eat junk food is likely to experience less illness. So while doctors, hospitals, and the latest medicine and treatments will be widely available and free for all to access, we may be able to scale back the healthcare sector. We may need fewer medical professionals and/or they could have a lighter workload (many healthcare professionals work far too many hours currently, leading to lower quality of life for them and medical mistakes for patients).

Additionally, due to the focus on environmental and preventative health aspects of people's lives, pharmaceutical use will be reduced. Medications will not be advertised, and they will be less likely to be prescribed as a default solution. People will have access to community support systems, including a focus on relaxation and rejuvenation and building relationships. This, combined with the opportunity to contribute in a meaningful way, may help many people find they no longer need medication for depression, anxiety disorders, or mood swings.

While the system of universal basic goods and services will potentially have a dramatic impact on the level of health and wellness in a community or region, it will also likely make a large impact on crime. Money-related crimes will not exist. Property theft will likely be nearly eliminated, as people will have little to gain by stealing anything. Drug abuse will be dealt with as a mental health and wellness issue. Driving while intoxicated will not exist, as nearly all forms of transportation will be autonomous. Violence and sex crimes will likely decrease as more children who are brought up in stable, caring, emotionally nourishing environments become adults and make up a larger percentage of society.

It is not outlandish to presume that through health and wellness interventions a significant portion of both disease and crime can be outright prevented. Additionally, longevity researchers postulate that through science and nutrition, the human lifespan could be dramatically extended if individuals are able to achieve optimal wellness conditions for extended periods of time.

Let us now look at how optimal conditions in other areas of our lives could be met in a sustainable fashion.

THE INDUSTRIAL SECTOR

In Chapter 3, we grouped multiple industries under the category "the industrial sector." In this chapter, we will break out four key areas—food, water, and agriculture; resources and manufacturing; transportation; and energy—so we can get more specific.

FOOD, WATER & AGRICULTURE

As discussed in Chapter 4, the capitalist system supports, incentivizes, and subsidizes conventional methods of growing food, including large-scale monocropping, tilling the soil, and the application of pesticides, herbicides, and fertilizers, with insufficient regard for the long-term detrimental effects these practices have on our environment and the climate. Without the profit motive, we are at liberty to implement high-yield, regenerative, sustainable systems for production of food and water. Three key areas of focus will be employed in the field of agriculture: localization, agroecology and regenerative agriculture, and automation.

Localization. Current modes of growing and processing food strain resources and contribute to pollution and greenhouse gas emissions. Complementing the idea of sustainable communities, future agricultural systems will grow food as close as possible to where it will be used to minimize resources expended for transportation, while also using the fewest resources possible in the production process.

Agroecology and Regenerative Agriculture. As mentioned in the previous chapter, agroecology and regenerative agriculture are critical to achieving ecological balance. While the two terms are often used ambiguously, and definitions differ depending on where in the world the practices are taking place, *agroecology* is an approach to agriculture that takes into account the entire ecosystem and impacts on it. It includes numerous methodologies and techniques for soil/environmental regeneration, holistic grazing practices, silvopasture, desert-greening, carbon farming/sequestration, and permaculture; it also entails a focus on specific cultures and how they relate to food and agriculture, and how soil health and agricultural practices affect the nutritional qualities of foods. *Regenerative agriculture* focuses on restoring soil health, sequestering carbon, healing the environment, increasing biodiversity, and fighting climate change through a variety of natural, technological, and restorative practices. Utilizing multiple systems to grow food in diverse environments, while simultaneously sequestering carbon back into the soil, is key to sustainable agriculture.

Automation. Technology can help engineer local agriculture and food-production systems that operate and are powered in a sustainable manner and can assist with the goals of regenerative agriculture and agroecology. Automated systems, such as FarmBot, will be used to help streamline and increase community and backyard food production; additionally, these systems are extremely efficient at conserving water, space, energy, and resources.

By implementing these three approaches, people will have access to an abundance of fresh, nutritious food grown by state-of-the-art technology that can effectively help regenerate the soil and the environment at the same time. Machine and chemical processes for removing carbon or other greenhouse gases from the atmosphere will work in tandem with the agricultural system, which will become largely carbon-negative.

Additionally, as with housing, retrofitting and repurposing structures like empty office buildings will become common; these stranded assets can be used to produce large amounts of food in high-density metropolitan areas.

RESOURCES & MANUFACTURING

As mentioned with both housing and agriculture, sustainable communities require localization to the extent possible. A central focus of manufacturing will be to ensure that the resources needed are sourced from sustainably produced materials and transported as little distance as possible, using renewable energy and employing carbon-sequestering processes. Therefore, as many resources as possible will be sourced locally, using regenerative methods to produce sustainably manufactured goods.

Of course, what works in one location may not work in another. Weather patterns and other conditions can vary dramatically, and solutions must be tailored to meet the demands of the local environment and climate. Specific conditions affect what can or cannot be grown, where energy or resources come from, what methods of transportation can be used, and so on. An effective, functioning moneyless society in Australia will work differently from one in Portugal, or from one in the Pacific Northwest. Part of the challenge is figuring out what types of systems work best in different regions and climates, and then replicating those systems in locations with similar conditions.

An additional focus is to be able to use the waste material from manufacturing as an input back into the environment or production line to create a circular economic model, as we discussed in the last chapter. Figure 17 shows how that model looks in a causal loop diagram:

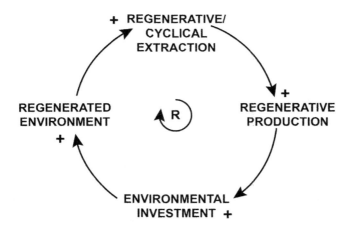

Figure 17: Causal Loop Diagram of Circular Production Model

In this simple clockwise cycle, we have a reinforcing loop starting with *regenerative/cyclical extraction* leading to *regenerative production* leading to *environmental investment* leading to a *regenerated environment*, and then returning to *regenerative/cyclical extraction* to begin the cycle again.

Hemp is a great example of a product that can be used as a regenerative element in many aspects of production. With the proper practices, growing hemp can help regenerate the environment, sequestering carbon into the soil and improving soil health and fertility. It is an extremely versatile agent for manufacturing and can be used in anything from building homes to manufacturing household items, making clothing, and even providing sustainable forms of concrete (hempcrete). The soil retains the benefits of growing the hemp crops (in the forms of sequestered carbon and improved soil quality) long after the hemp itself has been harvested. Over time, the more regenerative crops are grown in a plot of land, the better the soil gets. Carbon is also sequestered in the hemp itself, so when products are made with hemp, they are storing carbon that came out of the atmosphere.

Many goods will simply be manufactured, assembled, or 3D-printed at a local facility automatically and on-demand, without the person who ordered the item even seeing the process behind its production, much as print-on-demand books are published today. This type of consumer feedback—the simple process of ordering goods—along with the use of sensors to relay information along the *internet of things* (a network that enables sensors and devices to communicate with each other, also known as IoT), will likely constitute the majority of the consumer-feedback information needed for a mostly automated economy to function. Consumers simply give direct input to production facilities through their everyday use and ordering of products. For instance, if something is taken off a shelf at a grocery store, a sensor would collect that data and send it to the food production systems that calculate what and how much to produce and where the products go. The same system can occur when ordering online. Produce, for instance, could be automatically picked by a robot, ripe off the vine, from a local garden just blocks away, and then brought to your door using a small, renewably powered, electric delivery vehicle system within minutes. Depending on how many people order said produce, the production system itself would calculate how much to grow to satisfy demand in the future.

One major shift in manufacturing will be designing products to be easily repaired and upgraded. Two major principles to support this goal are *modularity*, the ability to put things together in standardized pieces, and *interoperability*, the ability of one system to work with or use parts of another system. Without the profit motive, competing interests are no longer incented to manufacture non-interchangeable parts for consumer goods or to design them for planned obsolescence, and can instead focus on creating sustainable products. For instance, a cracked screen on a smartphone would be easily and quickly replaced instead of the entire phone being discarded (and more likely the screen would be engineered not to break in the first place).

The process of developing sufficient open-source technology for use by society will likely result in large, public, digital libraries for open-source resources. These libraries will contain designs for products, processes for production, and other relevant information and tools. Publicly accessed facilities for production and part replacement for common goods will be available and free to use whenever needed. Of course, there may be specific educational requirements before a person is cleared for the operation of machinery, and there may also be community protocols for approving larger projects.

Larger, regional production centers will likely handle the manufacturing and assembly of more complex products, resource-intensive products, or products requiring materials that cannot be grown or sourced locally. Regions and nations will share their resources with one another as needed, and more sustainable materials will be sought for specific applications, such as finding a more sustainable replacement for cobalt in lithium-ion batteries (which is already happening[78]).

TRANSPORTATION

The ground-transportation industry is set to be completely overhauled within the next few decades. Owning a car full-time and driving it for only a small portion of the day is not likely to be a normal thing in the future. Autonomous vehicles powered by renewable energy sources are on course to make vehicle ownership obsolete by mid-century. Fleets of autonomous vehicles will be abundant and available at low cost and eventually free of charge. We will simply schedule a vehicle, like we do with Uber or Lyft today; it will pick us up, take us to our destination, and then go on to pick up its next passenger or sit somewhere and wait until it is summoned again. Additionally, the vehicles will be electric, zero-emission, light on resource use, built from sustainable materials, and highly modular.

Data from user-feedback systems and the internet of things will anticipate spikes in transportation needs and help ensure enough vehicles are available to meet peak demands. Also, since a large portion of the population will no longer need to travel to a job, there will be fewer commuters on the road in general, and traffic jams will likely be largely eliminated. We will also experience a smoother flow of traffic due in part to the capabilities of computer-controlled automobiles to maneuver and coordinate with each other more efficiently than human drivers can, thereby eliminating unnecessary slowdowns or stops that a human would have to make, such as at stop signs or red lights. Because humans cannot drive as efficiently as computers, human-driven cars will be obsolete and likely banned from public roads so that the more efficient self-driving technology can be utilized properly. This will eliminate most accidents and traffic deaths, and driving a car for personal pleasure will take place on a race-track away from public roads, akin to going horseback riding in the mountains.

Another nice side effect of the revolution in transportation is that many fewer parking lots will be needed. Currently the United States has somewhere between 800 million and two billion parking spaces for roughly 250 million cars, and surface lots cover more than 5 percent of all urban land.[79] In greater Los Angeles, if all the parking lots were condensed into one area, it would make a circle with a sixteen-mile diameter, stretching from Santa Monica to East Los Angeles.[80] Imagine what could be done with all that parking space! Eventually many places might not even have parking spaces—just drive-ways and passenger pick-up/drop-off areas. Parking lots will be placed in strategic locations for fleets of automated cars to sit and wait until they are summoned, but much of the space currently used for parking could be repurposed for regenerative agriculture, rehabilitating the natural environment, parks, energy production, housing, community centers, or many other things. Removing parking lots will also let more rainwater be absorbed back into the soil, which will help replenish ground-water in many areas.

Additionally, more electric trains and various types of renewably powered mass transportation will be employed. Other high-speed ground transportation technologies are likely to start being implemented as well, such as ET3 (evacuated tube transport technology) or Hyperloop. These high-speed, zero-emission transportation systems use magnetic levitation ("mag-lev") technology inside vacuum tubes to eliminate almost all aerodynamic friction and rolling resistance. Furthermore, they are hypothetically capable of achieving speeds in the many hundreds and possibly even thousands of miles per hour, without the use of fossil fuels, making them likely to offset the need for resource-intensive air travel. However, air travel too is likely to evolve into a more sustainable manifestation. Smaller aircraft powered by renewable energies are already coming on the scene. And if we could master antigravity technology? That may be the most significant contribution to environmental sustainability in human history. Sustainable antigravity capabilities would eliminate the need for most roads and bridges and thereby save massive amounts of resources, as well as potentially propel humanity to a new frontier in space exploration.

ENERGY

The restructuring of energy systems must effectively address two issues simultaneously:

- Producing enough energy from sustainable and ecologically friendly sources to meet demand, and
- Reducing demand through efficiency protocols, controlled economic contraction, and socioeconomic restructuring.

As we've already discussed, a large reduction in energy consumption will occur simply because much of the population will no longer have to produce "busywork" to satisfy the capitalist system. This will create a large reduction in fossil fuel use, as a portion of the economy will essentially close and never reopen. Without capitalist interests lobbying for the use of fossil fuels, we will have the capability of putting together a massive effort to transition over to a 100 percent renewably powered system relatively quickly.

The technologies we need to implement sustainable and lasting sources of energy—wind, solar, tidal, wave, geothermal, gravity, and hydroelectric—already exist and are simply waiting to be implemented on the scale necessary. Any single one of these will not solve our problems. Instead, a combination of these technologies will be the most effective and resilient, as shortfalls in one can be supplemented by others when needed.

One of the main hurdles with renewable energy is that often the best locations to generate power are not close to the locations where the energy is needed. For instance, the best locations for solar-energy production are in the sunniest places on the planet—deserts—where, not coincidentally, few people desire to live due to the inhospitable environment. Similar sentiments may be held for the windiest places, the most geothermally active, and so on. Often these places are long distances from large cities that need energy. Additionally, crowded cities often can't accommodate the installation of a variety of renewable-energy production devices, and for numerous reasons, cities are usually not the most ideal locations to generate power.

To address this problem, the most efficient solution may be a scaling-up and near-globalization of an ultra-high-voltage "super grid," a large-scale electric grid that connects multiple regions in a part of the world, enabling the transfer of renewably generated electricity over long distances. This type of grid is a key technology for worldwide adoption of renewable energy sources because it allows fluctuations in local sources to be smoothed out by accessing multiple other sources and transferring power between areas as needed, and it allows access to electricity in many places that currently do not have reliable sources for renewable electricity generation.

There are places, however, that are not conducive to being powered by a global energy super grid, such as isolated island nations. While it would not be difficult to supply many of these places with electricity during times when wind and solar energy are at their peak, finding ways to provide storage of energy during low-production times is the key to a 100 percent renewable system. However, even many isolated places have options such as using the force of gravity for energy storage. In this manner, mountains or even deep holes in the ground can be used for energy storage. During times of energy surplus, the renewable energy sources are used to mechanically lift heavy weights to higher locations that can later generate electricity by spinning turbines as they are lowered. The same principle can be used with water by pumping it up to reservoirs at higher altitudes at peak-production times, then using gravity and the force of running water to generate hydroelectric power when needed. These types of methods are already being implemented in numerous locations, such as El Hierro[81] in the Canary Islands. For a current list of locations that have achieved their 100 percent renewable-energy production goals, visit 100-percent.org/target-achieved/.

Another clever innovation to help meet our electricity-storage needs (and one that will likely be implemented on a large scale) is using idle vehicles. By tapping into electric vehicles' battery storage capabilities when the vehicles themselves are not in use, the cars can connect to smart power-supply stations that can provide the electrical grid with additional electricity during peak demand hours. This conveniently helps with one of the biggest setbacks to a 100 percent renewable electric grid—having enough battery storage available to meet peak demands, which often do not coincide with the times when energy production is at its highest.

In any case, there are numerous solutions for energy abundance in practically any area of the world. Utilizing a combination of these technologies will generally prove to be the most realistic solution.

GOVERNANCE & DECISION-MAKING

Finally, governance. How will we run this new moneyless society? The subject of governance and decision-making is a tricky one, because no matter what type of government exists in the future, there will be people who say that it does not work well or would work more efficiently if things were run differently in some way, shape, or form. However, whatever type of governance process the people in a moneyless society choose to exercise, if it is based on the principles outlined in this book, it is likely to exhibit a few specific qualities.

First, governance will likely be more participatory through better use of data systems and technology. People will be able to participate in government and the decision-making processes anytime, on their phone or computer, with streamlined, user-friendly software and databases that help large groups of people distill their thoughts down to relevant choices and dialogue. The Society Library is a project already attempting to build such a system. "All of society's points of view, all in one place" reads the homepage of the website (as of early 2022). To further clarify, on their mission and vision page, it details:

> The Society Library extracts arguments, claims, and evidence from various forms of media to compile databases which represent the ideas and arguments from all points of view starting with the most high-impact, persistent, and polarizing issues; to be visualized and made freely available to the public in a library. The long-term vision of the Society Library is to create a library of ideas not only on social and political subjects, but also philosophy, spirituality, and social values.
>
> . . .

> The Society Library's vision [is] to create a fully inten-
> tional, collaborative humanity which functionally negoti-
> ates ideological differences in a manner that maximizes
> freedom in being through access to information.

In other words, the project aims to give people the information
and tools they need to collaborate and cooperate effectively, on
a large scale, in a decentralized fashion, to aid in the progress
and overall well-being of humanity.

Second, many complex decisions in a moneyless society will
be better left to automated protocols or artificial intelligence
programs and computer algorithms, which can consider massive
amounts of data to make better decisions. AI programs can be
extremely fast at learning and are adept at coming to solutions
for many complex problems—such as the most efficient and
environmentally sound means of resource management and
distribution—far more accurately and effectively than humans
ever could. Decisions made by AI software could include things
like the number of autonomous vehicles that are needed to
satisfy the maximum demand at some future date, or what the
best types of regenerative crops to plant in a specific area are,
based on human demand, regional climate, specific soil composition, water availability, native/non-invasive species selection,
and other factors. (Caveat: There are known issues with current
AI; for example, searches about careers resulting in gender-
biased images and facial-recognition tools having trouble iden-
tifying people with dark skin. So it's almost certain there are
other biases we need to continue weeding out. Remember,
everything is interrelated, so technology and social justice are
connected.)

Third, the absence of financial budgets and conflicting
capitalist interests, along with the elimination of numerous rules

and regulations in place to contain capitalism-gone-wild, will eliminate a large portion of the political friction that exists in large-scale decision-making today. Without the monetary system and corporate lobbying to hinder and curtail progress, many of the money- and property-related interests that are in direct conflict with the well-being of people and the environment will cease to exist. Additionally, resources that are currently being directed to people and corporations that don't need them will finally be able to go to the people and places where they are needed the most.

Fourth, upgrades to other industries will also make many governmental bodies nearly or completely nonexistent. With automated vehicles and mass transit as the new normal, the need for driver licensing is eliminated, drastically reducing the need for the Department of Motor Vehicles. Building codes for new construction will be incorporated into the software for 3D printing or the construction programs themselves, automatically ensuring that construction projects meet certain specified structural integrity requirements.

Finally, industries, communities, regions, and sectors will all likely operate more autonomously than they do today, given the increased role in decision-making each would have. The same types of tools that the Society Library hopes to provide to individuals will likely also aid any governing bodies in their interactions as well as potentially facilitate mutual aid agreements between parties. This aspect of interconnection will provide a high level of antifragility by giving such entities or regions more leeway to adjust and correct in an emergency or shock.

There are a number of governance models that could evolve, such as sociocracy or anarcho-syndicalism. Sociocracy, for example, utilizes small groups, called circles, to promote equality and help foster self-governance. Anarcho-syndicalism advocates for worker self-management and cooperation/mutual aid agreements between autonomous communities. The models we discuss in the next chapter will likely be suitable to a sociocratic governance method or something similar. It will be interesting to see what evolves.

BUT HOW DO WE GET THERE?

As you can see, while we have laid out a general framework for the systemic operations of a functioning moneyless society, there is still much to figure out about the details of how the individual parts and components will function and integrate with one another. Research needs to be done, experiments need to take place, people need to come together, relationships need to be cemented, and organizations need to be formed. We need to find out what works, how it works, where it works, why it works, and then replicate it in as many situations as we can.

And this brings us to one of the major questions I hear regarding this subject: How could we possibly transition to this type of society? We will explore some of the potential answers to this question in the next chapter.

CHAPTER 7

TRANSITIONING TO A MONEYLESS SOCIETY

If machines produce everything we need, the outcome will depend on how things are distributed. Everyone can enjoy a life of luxurious leisure if the machine-produced wealth is shared, or most people can end up miserably poor if the machine-owners successfully lobby against wealth redistribution. So far, the trend seems to be toward the second option, with technology driving ever-increasing inequality.

STEPHEN HAWKING

Much like a caterpillar about to wrap itself in a chrysalis, we humans have a small window of opportunity to build a new society and emerge as a civilization that operates harmoniously with our natural world. If a caterpillar does not build a chrysalis and metamorphose into a butterfly, it will die. The same is true for humans. If we do not take the limited chance we have and transform our civilization into something that operates synergistically with our biosphere, then we as a species will die.

When picturing our capitalist society making a transition to a moneyless society, it's realistic to see it as a process that will be achieved relatively quickly on a smaller, networked scale as proof-of-concept demonstrations, and then grow and branch out from there. On a large or global scale, a smooth transition to a moneyless society is possible for a good portion of society if the needed systems and structures can be developed and implemented *before* any such transition.

In this chapter, we will take the principles laid out in Chapter 5 and the vision of future systems from Chapter 6 and organize them into what I call *constructive elements* for building a functioning moneyless society. We'll also look at how the transition is likely to unfold and learn about some of the organizations already moving toward that transition.

THE FOUR CONSTRUCTIVE ELEMENTS

Before any large-scale transition to a moneyless society can occur, four constructive elements need to be intentionally implemented, at least in part:

- A system of universal basic goods and services,
- Automation protocols for manufacturing and resource generation,
- A sustainable/circular economy, and
- Collective ownership of the means of production, likely via cooperatives.

We've talked about the first three in some detail already, so I'll simply summarize them here, and we'll dig into the fourth constructive element at greater length.

CONSTRUCTIVE ELEMENT 1: UNIVERSAL BASIC GOODS & SERVICES

Kickstarting the beginnings of a moneyless society will take the implementation of a system to provide universal basic goods and services (UBGS), as we described in Chapter 5, to at least a portion of the population. Essentially, this idea ensures that people receive for free what they need to operate, survive, and thrive: food, housing, clothing, household goods, electricity, computers, internet access, and so on. (Let me reiterate that this concept is similar to but fundamentally different from the concept of universal basic income, in which people receive money instead of the actual goods and services that are needed.)

CONSTRUCTIVE ELEMENT 2: AUTOMATION & TECHNOLOGY

Technology has given us the world we live in—computers, cars, dishwashers, solar panels, toilets—and can increase the standard of living for anyone with access to it. In a moneyless society, our goal is to use technology to increase the standard of living for *everyone*. Not only can technology and automation eliminate vast amounts of human labor, but they can help us solve problems that were previously unsolvable. The more automation and technology can be implemented in ways that foster cooperation, abundance, and sustainability, the better.

However, to effectively leverage technology's potential, it behooves us to prevent competitive interests from hoarding useful technologies. Without capitalism's constraints, we are free to share innovations openly and use technology and automation in ways that truly benefit people and the environment. Robotics, automated production and delivery systems, and the development of artificial intelligence to assist with complex problem-solving are all included in this element.

Additionally, technology can be used in feedback and decision-making processes. Automated sensors and mechanisms that gather and transmit data within an internet of things (IoT) will act as the lifeblood to the various production systems. Together with data processing and exchange, sensor-driven IoT production will effectively replace the price mechanism and trade systems of the past. Technology will also be used to engage the public in decision-making, supporting the development and implementation of cooperative and democratically controlled systems. Incomprehensible amounts of data will be recorded and exchanged within and between myriad systems, most of which will silently occur in the background, to help facilitate the day-to-day operations of society.

CONSTRUCTIVE ELEMENT 3: SUSTAINABLE/CIRCULAR ECONOMY

A sustainable/circular economy is one in which all waste products are utilized for other purposes or are eliminated entirely and there exists a large focus on reuse and regeneration.

In this economy, manufacturing is structured so that any unused, leftover, or extra materials are somehow utilized in a productive fashion. And other sustainable practices, such as reuse, recycling, upcycling, repurposing, and localization, contribute to sustainability and lessen the environmental cost of a community or venture.

Additionally, there is adequate investment back into the environment in the form of regenerative agriculture or similar means to ensure that our natural world keeps producing enough resources and raw materials to meet society's needs. A focus on regenerative agriculture also provides a degree of sovereignty over food and resources, self-sufficiency, and a baseline regenerative capacity, not to mention marketable commodities and a source of income during the transitional period.

CONSTRUCTIVE ELEMENT 4:
COOPERATION & COOPERATIVES

Finally, if we are to progress beyond capitalism's competitive dynamics, then we must start acting in more cooperative ways, on both individual and collective levels. To do so, we must adopt business models capable of fostering cooperation while functioning within our existing economic and business framework. Fortunately, there is a reasonably flexible business model already in existence with agreements, language, and structure similar to those a moneyless society will need: the cooperative.

The collective-ownership model of cooperatives is versatile enough to suit a wide variety of purposes and possesses the potential to incorporate the concepts needed for a moneyless society. We will likely see many more of these democratic, community-focused ownership and management structures take hold as more sustainable and egalitarian models gain popularity in the years to come.

What Is a Cooperative?

A *cooperative*, or "co-op," is a type of business owned and democratically controlled by the people who work for the company and/or use its services. These individuals are called *members* or *member-owners* and they reap benefits from the co-op in two important ways:
- Receiving services and products that they need, and
- Receiving profits (at least in today's world), which are distributed to all members.

Whereas regular corporations are driven primarily by generating profit for the owners or shareholders, co-ops give their member-owners more influence on the organization's decision-making processes and ensure that everyone involved receives fair dividends for their efforts. In this atmosphere, workers try hard for the company to succeed, because they do not work *for* the company—they *are* the company. They all *own* the company, so they work for themselves.

The concept of democratic worker-ownership of companies is not novel and has its history in the ideas of the Enlightenment. The cooperative model is essentially nothing more than an extension of the idea of democracy in the one place people spend most of their adult lives: work.

Co-ops aren't limited to any one industry, niche, or region— they thrive in both rural and urban areas, and they can be both for-profit and nonprofit organizations. Using cooperatives to empower disadvantaged communities is already gaining traction in the United States and around the globe. The Arizmendi Bakery cooperative in the San Francisco Bay Area now has multiple locations implementing their worker-owned model and is currently expanding into Los Angeles. The Evergreen Cooperatives of Cleveland (Ohio) have helped numerous communities in the area through multiple worker-owned businesses, including a solar installation company, a hydroponics farm, and a laundry facility. Cooperation Jackson in Mississippi is another emerging network of cooperatives. Cooperative federations, groups of cooperatives that work together within a greater organizational structure, have the capacity to create cooperative ecosystems that would normalize the practice of cooperation and democracy in an otherwise competitive marketplace.

While there are many forms of cooperatives, depending on their purpose and location, most share certain characteristics. The International Cooperative Alliance has defined seven cooperative principles that most co-ops generally follow:[82]

- Voluntary and open membership
- Democratic member control

- Member economic participation
- Autonomy and independence
- Education, training, and information
- Cooperation among cooperatives
- Concern for community

Not coincidentally—because they are based on equity and cooperation—many of the principles in cooperatives align nicely with the principles required to build a moneyless society. The eventual goal is to align the cooperative principles with the purpose of building the infrastructure necessary for creating a technologically abundant, sustainable post-scarcity society.

Types of Cooperatives

Cooperatives are more common than you may think. Roughly thirty thousand cooperatives exist in the US economy alone, spanning multiple sectors. Worldwide, three million cooperatives exist, which serve more than a billion members and account for 12 percent of the world's employed population.[83] The Associated Press, Sunkist, Ocean Spray, Land O'Lakes, and Ace Hardware are, in fact, all successful cooperatives. If structured properly, co-ops can provide almost every imaginable service and product. Here are the most common forms of cooperatives:

Producer Cooperatives. Producer co-ops are usually used by members who produce similar items in separate enterprises to help leverage greater negotiating power and control prices. These cooperatives may provide supplies, marketing, processing, or insurance, among other services. Producer co-ops may be developed for artist studios, fishing boats, or any number of other industries, and are especially common in livestock and agricultural products. Land O'Lakes (the butter company) is a farmer-owned producer co-op that's been around since 1921. Ocean Spray and Sunkist are also producer cooperatives.

Consumer Cooperatives. These co-ops are owned by the people who buy from the co-op, which can provide nearly anything people want—from groceries to electricity to healthcare. Consumer cooperatives can be small—a food-buying club in a rural village—or large, multimillion-dollar enterprises, such as REI or the Spanish supermarket chain Eroski, a worker-consumer co-op that is part of the Mondragon Corporation. Even some of today's insurance companies operate like consumer co-ops. Mutual insurance companies—think Mutual of Omaha—are owned by the policyholders, who receive dividends (or a return of premium) when the company prospers.

Credit Unions. Credit unions are essentially a form of consumer cooperative; every person who deposits money into a credit union account is a member-owner. The member-owners generally share a common characteristic, such as having the same employer, belonging to the same organization, or living in the same community.

Housing Cooperatives. A housing cooperative is a corporation created to purchase a group housing structure, where each member holds shares of the corporation and is entitled to one housing unit. Members often participate democratically in the management of the property as well. Size and complexity range from small developments with several units to large properties with full-time employees and hundreds of units run by boards of directors or similar committees.

Retail or Purchasing Cooperatives. In this type of co-op, independent business owners form an organization to increase efficiency in purchasing supplies and/or providing services; these are sometimes called *shared service cooperatives*. This type of co-op includes several businesses you may recognize, such as Ace Hardware and Carpet One.

Social Cooperatives. This emerging type of cooperative

has a specific social mission, such as improving working conditions for women or providing healthcare to a community. These are common in Italy and several other countries, and may also function and be classified as other types of cooperatives in this list as well.

Worker Cooperatives. These businesses are owned by some or all workers. Worker co-ops are popular with, for example, attorneys, engineers, restaurants, and day care centers. Both the Arizmendi Bakery in the Bay Area and the Evergreen Cooperative in Ohio are worker cooperatives.

Benefits of Worker Cooperatives

While some cooperative models, such as consumer cooperatives and producer cooperatives, incorporate more traditional aspects of the capitalist model—including, but not limited to, the employee-employer relationship—worker cooperatives distribute ownership of the company among the workers themselves and therefore generally exhibit an equity/ownership model that other cooperative models may lack.

Since the workers control the firm, they tend to make decisions that benefit all workers, not just upper management. They keep income inequality in check by instituting salary caps. During market crashes and times of crisis, these cooperatives usually opt to cut hours and wages across the board rather than lay off workers. If some enterprises become obsolete over time, the cooperative model helps workers move to different jobs in the cooperative ecosystem where there is more demand for labor. And since cooperatives' worker-owners often reside locally, they tend not to make decisions that will harm the environment around them.

Interestingly (and unsurprisingly), cooperatives have recently been gaining footholds in some capitalist-dominated markets.

Mondragon is the largest cooperative organization in the world, housing ninety-five individual cooperatives under its umbrella. They have created their own university, housing for their worker-members, their own major grocery store chain (Eroski, mentioned above), and a credit union with complete financial services. As one of Europe's leading producers of technological equipment for solar module manufacturing, they've also become a technology and manufacturing powerhouse. Additionally, Mondragon is forging the networks needed to gain power in the political sphere as well as potentially overshadow capitalism in areas where it is becoming a less dominant socioeconomic model.

COMBINING THE CONSTRUCTIVE ELEMENTS

These four constructive elements combine to help create the social, ecological, and economic prosperity at the heart of our moneyless society systems diagram in Chapter 6. Several drivers integrate these elements into a powerful catalyst for change:

Community. The physical embodiment of the constructive elements will likely manifest in sustainable, self-sufficient, highly automated, democratically run "live-work-play" communities. These communities will be founded upon equal ownership of the means of production (as well as any buildings, homes, or infrastructure), and everyone involved will receive the benefits from the production of goods within the community. Cooperatives and communities will serve as a home base and support system for member-owners as well as a demonstration and example for others to see how the universal basic goods and services (UBGS) system functions in real life.

Purpose. Cooperatively owned businesses and/or communities will coalesce around the initial purpose of providing members of the community with UBGS. A cooperative tasked with taking care of the needs of its members can serve that purpose without the threat of having to constantly produce a return for its investors. Besides the basic labor and income needed to operate within the framework of capitalism for the time being, any other funding, income, or effort can be directed toward creating the capabilities of producing goods and services for free within the framework of the community.

Collaboration. As an effective strategy for transitioning to a moneyless society, cooperatives will begin to collaborate, which will contribute to a snowball effect. As worker-owner cooperatives start to intertwine with communities, the distinct separation between one's work, one's social life, and one's home life will start to fade. A person's community also becomes their work, and the people in the community start to serve each other's needs. A network of thriving cooperatives, functioning without the constraints of competitive capitalist models, will also possess a much greater capacity to adapt, evolve, partner, communicate effectively, approach issues objectively, and correct internal problems.

Scale. As more cooperative businesses are formed and network with each other, the capacity for cooperatives to provide necessities (and more) for free to their members will grow. As time goes on, and as networks of cooperatives and their capabilities expand, an abundance of goods and services will become available to members. Numerous communities will eventually have their own means of producing everyday goods and necessities with resources that are sourced regeneratively and locally or within a close network of communities. With automation and technology that eliminates unnecessary labor and streamlines the production and delivery processes, it may only take a small number of cooperatives working together before a spectrum of universal basic goods and services can be provided to the member-owners free of charge, providing them with a quality of life and community support comparable to or better than any found in modern society.

When visitors can experience the principles and systems discussed in this book firsthand, they will sense that the current economic system is becoming obsolete. They will experience a way of life that operates more harmoniously with the natural inclinations of both humans and the planet. These types of communities will help spread the idea of sustainable living, leading to the formation of new communities and cooperatives and the building of more automated production systems. This expansion will also help round out the UBGS system to include more everyday items.

The potential exists for an eventual network of cooperative communities to span the globe, so that if members wanted to, they could travel and stay in various cooperative facilities, attend different programs, learn new skills, help with various projects, and develop new relationships—all while working within the system of networked cooperatives and receiving universal basic goods and services wherever they go.

THE FIVE STAGES OF TRANSITION

What does the timeline of events look like in the transition to a moneyless society? Unless there is some sort of top-down government intervention (and there probably won't be), five distinct stages of the transition to a moneyless society will likely occur.

STAGE 1: INCREASING AWARENESS

Increasing awareness is the stage we are in now (hence the reason for this book). Many people know there is a problem with our current economic system, but relatively few can pinpoint the root causes and even fewer the solutions. This book is designed to help create awareness and move us past the first stage of transition. When a large enough percentage of the population is aware of the problem and ready to do something about it, we can start to act at a scale that has a chance of making a difference.

Younger generations, in particular, are more likely to adopt sustainable, progressive practices and lifestyles. In the face of the openly hostile market economy, younger people—unable to find meaningful work or afford a home and faced with a lifetime of climate-related disasters to look forward to—are more likely to embrace equal-ownership cooperative models both in work and at home, to combine forces and mitigate whatever damage they can. Younger generations also tend to be more at ease with technology and will likely be drawn to "smart cities" that can revolutionize the ways we live, work, and interact. These ingredients are all catalysts for the creation of new systems and structures.

Fortunately, the public is starting to see that the situation cannot be ignored any longer, and people are beginning to demand significant change. As time goes on, and as more millennials (born between 1980 and 1996) and their younger counterparts step into positions of power, the practices we advocate in this book are more likely to become more commonplace and integrated into society.

STAGE 2: PLANNING, FORMATION, ORGANIZATION & MOBILIZATION

The second stage is the beginning of large-scale grassroots mobilization. Numerous groups of ordinary individuals come together, online and in person, and collectively decide to take on the project of supplying themselves, either as a community or group of communities, with universal basic goods and services. Cooperatives, other intentionally created businesses, and equitable-ownership live-work-play communities are formed with the goal and purpose of working together to build a UBGS system that will be scalable, duplicable, highly automated, and sustainably produced.

In this stage, the focus is on organization, structure, planning, developing protocols, and generally moving people in the right direction. This stage is about building relationships, forming entities, creating frameworks, making agreements, collecting resources, making plans, and taking action. This includes finding the people who have the skills and connections necessary to build the new economic systems, and getting them on the same page, focused on creating a network of cooperatives to provide the infrastructure necessary for universal basic goods and services. Once the organizational and planning phase is sufficiently developed, we are prepared to execute the plans.

STAGE 3: PHYSICAL INFRASTRUCTURE & SYSTEMS BUILDING

In Stage 3, we build infrastructure. The cooperatives that were established in Stage 2 have now matured and networked to a degree that enables them to begin to provide universal basic goods and services to their members. In this stage, a large degree of self-sufficiency is achieved in sourcing and manufacturing most products. Many services, such as childcare, healthcare, and education, are beginning to be provided within the cooperative network.

The demonstration and experimental communities that were formed in Stage 2 are now firmly established and actively assisting one another. The first "mostly moneyless" cooperative communities come online and focus on working out the kinks, eventually acting as models for others to follow. Entire small cities or towns are formed with or converting to post-scarcity principles. Substantial portions of the social systems and economies within these communities are focused on achieving carbon-negative production and manufacturing, large-scale regenerative agriculture, and other very low/zero-emissions or carbon-sequestering infrastructure.

Most necessities, such as food, water, housing, electricity, and local transportation, are now provided for community members free of charge. At this point, a significant portion of member-owners can survive within the cooperative network without having to maintain an outside job or source of income.

STAGE 4: EXPANSION, LARGE-SCALE ADOPTION & IMPLEMENTATION

In Stage 4, the UBGS/cooperative model becomes the preferred economic mode of production and begins to eclipse traditional capitalist models and businesses. This will occur after a critical mass is reached in the percentage of populations that adopt this new and improved way of life. Past observances and studies have shown that the "tipping point" necessary for large social change usually takes place around the 25 percent mark.[84]

At this point, automation is being heavily implemented.

New, large cities with new types of "smart" infrastructure are being built from the ground up. User-friendly interfaces are developed to facilitate democratic-consensus-hybrid decision-making, and IoT data organization systems become fully integrated into communities and production models. Automated manufacturing of many goods and services comes online; most goods and services are free to use or access for all members of the co-op network. Most people within the cooperative network can now fully rely on the cooperative system to survive.

This stage is focused on expanding the scope and scale of the UBGS system, both physically and digitally, while making all information and designs for production and manufacturing processes open source and free to use. With the basic infrastructure and designs in place to provide initial UBGS, more members, communities, businesses, and resources can now be integrated into the cooperative network.

The more the network expands, the more the network can work cooperatively to produce a full array of universal basic goods and services. The ultimate goal is to provide as many services, products, and experiences for members as is possible within the network, while instituting sustainable and regenerative practices. At this stage, world leaders are also beginning to make plans to transition to a global moneyless society.

STAGE 5: FULL-SCALE INTEGRATION & WINDING DOWN OF CAPITALISM

In the final integration stage, a fully functional moneyless society and UBGS system are coming into place, and a controlled winding down of capitalist structures commences. National governments now cooperate fully in open-source development and expansion of the UBGS system. All necessities, goods, and services can now be provided for free for anyone, anywhere, rendering money, currency, the formal debt system, and commercial trade obsolete.

Decisions regarding resource management are directed through computer algorithms and direct user-feedback mechanisms, including data from automatic sensors and democratic/consensus decision-making computer applications. Dangerous and monotonous labor is fully automated. Near 100 percent sustainable, regenerative, carbon-negative living and production are achieved globally.

Workloads and salaries are voluntarily and intentionally reduced over time and replaced by an increasing supply of universal basic goods and services. Once a certain threshold within the cooperative-community network is reached whereby automated, regenerative production systems can be expanded using robotics or AI and minimal labor, a large portion of the population can be rapidly transitioned to the UBGS system without a corresponding increase in the labor needed to provide the necessities. The speed and scale of additional implementation of automation, along with other environmental factors (such as weather and climate change) will be a large determinant of how many people the growing UBGS system can support and the rate of growth that can be supported at any given time.

Eventually, within this final transitional stage, a controlled contraction and winding down of the capitalist system will need to occur. It is possible that at some point in this transition some or all of the remaining capitalist businesses will collapse at a systemic level, because they no longer have the activity, workforce, or consumer base necessary to support their perpetuation. This event has the potential to throw the population still dependent upon the capitalist system into an economic collapse and create much unnecessary turmoil. To avoid large-scale civil unrest, such a scenario must be effectively anticipated, including developing a plan for creating the capacity to support, orient, and organize a massive influx of new arrivals into the UBGS system.

Lastly, and as a caution, local and regional plans and policies must consider the culture, wishes, and values of each community and the individuals who live there, their relative contexts and relationships, their environment and history, and the geography of the surrounding areas. Implementing universal solutions in complex systems without taking local and cultural factors into account will backfire and create rejection, hostility, and division. Paying close attention to local needs, desires, cultures, and traditions—especially those of immigrants, marginalized or disadvantaged community members, Indigenous peoples, and, yes, even capitalists—is critical in bringing about the integration of cooperative structures and practices that work for everyone.

TRANSITIONAL MOVEMENTS & ORGANIZATIONS

Numerous people have already put in years of work to realize the goal of transitioning to a moneyless society. From movies to movements to machines, for decades people and organizations have been creating systems, compiling information, and working on projects propelling us in the direction of building a new, free world. Let us take a brief look at a few of these movements, initiatives, and organizations.

JACQUE FRESCO & THE VENUS PROJECT

Based at a twenty-one-acre center in Venus, Florida, The Venus Project is the brainchild of the late Jacque Fresco, author, structural engineer, industrial designer, and futurist. It proposes a socioeconomic model called a *resource-based economy (RBE)* that utilizes the most current technological and scientific advances to provide the highest possible living standard for all people on Earth.

This nonprofit organization's socioeconomic model incorporates natural resource management, sustainable cities and values, energy efficiency, collective farms, and advanced automation driven by social cooperation and scientific methodology. It emphasizes the reassessment and overhauling of all aspects of human society—from our values, education, and urban design to how we relate to nature and one another. It would not be an overstatement to say that The Venus Project has reignited a modern passion for futurism and egalitarianism in many individuals.

For more information, visit TheVenusProject.com.

PETER JOSEPH & THE ZEITGEIST MOVEMENT

Peter Joseph is a filmmaker, musician, author, activist, public speaker, and creator of the *Zeitgeist* film trilogy. His first film, *Zeitgeist: The Movie* (which is unrelated to the movement and was originally intended as a performance piece not for release to the general public), went viral and garnered a great deal of criticism due to some of the film's widely disputed views concerning religion and 9/11. His second film, however, *Zeitgeist: Addendum*, focused on a comprehensive critique of capitalism and the monetary system, and highlighted the solutions proposed by The Venus Project as an alternative to our modern socioeconomic system. This movie also went viral and became the catalyst for the creation of The Zeitgeist Movement (TZM), which is now a global grassroots movement. With many thousands of members and chapters in over seventy countries, TZM advocates transitioning to a resource-based economy and, like The Venus Project, recommends implementation of sustainable ecology and the scientific administration of society.

After initially partnering with and then splitting from The Venus Project in the early 2010s, Peter Joseph expanded upon the idea of a resource-based economy to include the premise of "natural law," emphasizing the flexibility of systems and structures based on our current understandings of science and nature. He coined the term *natural law resource-based economy (NLRBE)*, the core of The Zeitgeist Movement's proposed social mechanism, which is based on public interaction facilitated by programmed, open-access systems that enhance a constant dynamic feedback exchange. Overall, much like The Venus Project's RBE model, the aim of the NLRBE model is to increase quality of life for all humans while maintaining sustainability in the long run by means of optimized industrial efficiency.

For more information, visit TheZeitgeistMovement.com.

THE AURAVANA PROJECT

Seemingly picking up where The Venus Project and The Zeitgeist Movement left off, Travis Grant and Elizabeth Reizinger, the driving force behind the Auravana Project, have created a vast body of work that details much of the integration and functionality of the principles and systems found in this book when applied to a large-scale society. The project lays out the blueprints of how such a society might operate, and creates systems and standards for such. According to their website, they seek "to develop a society that is reasonably automated, contribution-based, operates without trade or coercion, and meets global human need fulfillment requirements within the carrying capacity of the ecology." Volumes of work, containing thousands of pages of societal planning materials, CAD drawings, videos, architectural designs for circular communities with regenerative agriculture, spreadsheets with details of similar organizations, and more, can be found on their website for free.

For more information, visit auravana.org.

ONE COMMUNITY GLOBAL

Founded by Jae Sabol in 2010, One Community Global is a 100 percent volunteer-run nonprofit and nongovernmental organization with the goal of developing sustainable, open-source communities. It currently operates as a sustainability think tank with the goal of designing and building seven different communal-living village models of fifteen to one hundred residences as prototypes for self-sufficient communities to be built around the world. Each village model will represent a different ultra-affordable, eco-friendly development methodology that can be combined with their other open-source components, such as food, energy, and education.

Like The Venus Project, One Community Global firmly believes that the sharing of resources is significantly more ecologically sustainable, and free sharing of ideas fosters enhanced efficiency, ingenuity, and collaboration. They deemphasize consumerism and strongly promote community-based decision-making when creating, replacing, upgrading, or purchasing necessities such as food, energy, housing, and education. This consequently reduces waste, encourages cooperation, and enhances an integrated environment where relationships are preferred to accumulation of material possessions.

For more information, visit OneCommunityGlobal.org.

OPEN SOURCE ECOLOGY

Founded by Marcin Jakubowski in 2003, Open Source Ecology (OSE) aims to create a collaborative economic platform that optimizes development, production, and distribution—via open-source collaboration—to accelerate innovation to unprecedented levels. Essentially, OSE is a network of farmers, engineers, architects, students, and supporters who are developing a set of open-source blueprints for what is known as the Global Village Construction Set (GVCS), a set of the fifty most important machines essential to modern life. This set of machines includes everything from an oven to a circuit maker to a fully operational motor vehicle. Open Source Ecology intends to build and open-source not just individual machines but machine construction systems that can be used to build any machine whatsoever. This allows anyone with the proper skills, resources, and tools to build, maintain, and even sell these machines at a fraction of what they cost today. Open Source Ecology believes the power these machines give people has the ability to free them from material constraints and ultimately—by tapping their autonomy, mastery, and purpose—unleash their full human potential.

For more information, visit OpenSourceEcology.org.

MONEYLESS SOCIETY

Moneyless Society, our organization, began in 2013 as a simple website and in 2021 became a 501(c)(3) nonprofit. As a growing social movement, we just surpassed 250,000 Facebook followers and have an active YouTube channel. We now boast a volunteer team of nearly fifty people, and as we print this book, we are recording the second season of the Moneyless Society podcast, which can be found on all the major podcast streaming platforms. We have several projects in the works, including a full-length documentary film and Magnova.space, a website/hub for collaboratively solving global problems and democratizing the means of production.

Currently, we are working with an undisclosed owner of a large parcel of land in the Rust Belt area to help develop a regenerative agriculture and community project, and we are in the beginning stages of developing a smaller agricultural property in San Diego County. We are also in the preliminary planning and due-diligence phases of creating a community like the ones we described earlier in this chapter. Our overall aim is to form the beginnings of a functional UBGS network in the United States by the year 2030.

If you would like more information, please visit our website: MoneylessSociety.com. If you would like to reach us, or are interested in contributing to one of our many projects, please email us at contact@MoneylessSociety.com.

YES, WE CAN DO IT

On first reading, these ideas may seem overwhelming and intimidating, but the more you learn about this subject, the more you will see that the systems and structures we describe here are in fact possible, and that we have the technology and capabilities to achieve them. A protopian society is realistic, pragmatic, and within reach. It can and will be built one brick at a time, one step at a time, by people just like us. Real people are working on it now. Care to join us?

For additional resources and information on more projects, people, and organizations helping move us to a moneyless society, please see Appendix A.

CHAPTER 8

OBJECTIONS

Progress is impossible without change; and those who cannot change their minds cannot change anything.

GEORGE BERNARD SHAW

If there is one thing that I have heard time and time again, it is that the ideas in this book won't work, followed by sometimes lengthy, sometimes flimsy, explanations why. While this chapter will not address every issue that naysayers bring up, I feel it presents a well-rounded explanation of and rebuttal to some of the most common objections.

OBJECTION 1: HUMANS NEED MONETARY INCENTIVES

People are often intrigued by the notion of a moneyless society, but one of the most common arguments against it is the lack of monetary incentive for people to work. The concept of working without expecting a monetary reward seems alien to many people, so they have trouble wrapping their heads around alternatives to getting paid for work.

As we discussed in Chapter 6, in a moneyless society, people will still be incentivized to work through the mechanism of positive reinforcement. However, instead of positive reinforcement in the form of money, people will receive it directly, in the form of concrete benefits to the community, praise and gratitude, relationships, and security.

In Abraham Maslow's familiar hierarchy of needs, unsatisfied needs are the motivator of human behavior. His theory identifies five levels of basic needs—physiological, safety, belonging and love, esteem, and self-actualization—arrayed in a hierarchical pyramid with physiological at the bottom and self-actualization at the top. In this model, after one level is satisfied, its influence on behavior decreases, and the next higher level becomes the foremost motivator. In recent years it has been argued these needs should not be organized as a strict hierarchy. For example, a person can still feel a need for love and belonging even without having all their physical needs met. Nonetheless, an unmet need is a motivator.

In our current market society—where practically everything is commodified and traded—money has become understandably confounded with motivation, because it is required for individuals, communities, and even entire nations to realize practically all their needs. While it's true that "money can't buy you love," even such things as "affection" and "community" are more easily obtained when you have funds to take someone on a date and enough money to make a down payment on a house in your desired neighborhood. In other words, money can not only help you access most needs, it can also become a barrier to them.

In a moneyless society, with necessities (especially physiological and security needs) already provided, money is removed as both motivator and barrier. People will simply be influenced by the other motivators, such as love and belonging, esteem, and self-actualization. Human beings are expansional, dynamic creatures, constantly on the lookout for ways to contribute, grow, evolve, and experience life. We value progress and contribution; we thrive when we get to participate in dynamic, conscious evolution—and we have the opportunity to do that right now, in our lives, and in our communities, if we choose to do so. The most exciting part is that the physical results, the relationships, and the tangible benefits in real life are far better motivators and are far more fulfilling than money itself or simple material wealth ever can be.

The truth is, monetary incentives are growing increasingly ineffective, confounding employers in particular. Multiple studies have shown that after a certain threshold, financial rewards have the opposite effect from what is expected. In his book *Drive: The Surprising Truth about What Motivates Us*,[85] Daniel Pink contends,

> Rewards can perform a weird sort of behavioral alchemy: They can transform an interesting task into a drudge. They can turn play into work. And by diminishing intrinsic motivation, they can send performance, creativity, and even upstanding behavior toppling like dominoes.

Have you ever had a hobby you enjoyed doing for free, but when you started doing it for a living, you found you no longer enjoyed it as much? Money gets in the way of and clouds the other positive reinforcement that we would naturally derive from these sorts of tasks. In fact, heavily relying on compensation promotes bad behavior, such as cheating and short-term thinking, rather than the results desired.

For many of us, especially the younger generations, our internal barometers are flashing red that something is wrong with the current approach. A shift in social values is becoming apparent: workers are valuing autonomy and purpose as well as money. One main indicator of this social shift is how millennials have been transforming the workplace. In 2016, research by Gallup[86] found that millennials want a job that provides more than a paycheck or "job satisfaction." They want a job that conveys meaning and offers personal development. They do not want to work for institutions that do not encourage them to reach their greatest potential, even if that means they must constantly change jobs.

But on a less philosophical, more practical level, without being paid, why would anyone perform "yucky" jobs like garbage collector and portable toilet cleaner? Fair question. First, the long-term goal is to automate unpleasant, mundane, repetitive jobs to the extent possible; this automation is key to a functional, large-scale moneyless society. But automation is not something that we can implement overnight, so there will be an interim period where these jobs still need to be performed. During the transitional period, people will still be paid to work. Over time, as automation and the UBGS system are implemented, both pay and workloads will be reduced. Ultimately, any tasks that cannot be automated will simply be divided up between volunteers to keep the system functioning in its entirety.

OBJECTION 2: HUMANS ARE TOO LAZY

To extend the objection above, another concern is that once everyone's basic needs are taken care of, there will be those who would take advantage of the system and become lazy, abusing the system and putting undue stress and responsibility on the people who contribute their time and effort to society. This objection basically argues that without the constant threat of homelessness or starvation, we'd be left with a society of loafers and slackers. But is this true? Would too many people just sit on the beach and drink margaritas or become couch potatoes, playing video games and watching Netflix every day?

Indeed, there may be some people who are content "slacking," but most people will likely get bored and aspire to achieve something more. If there are still problems (and there will always be problems in this world), then there will also be people who will work to solve them. People also have an inherent desire to contribute and make a difference in others' lives. The decision to help others comes naturally for many individuals when their own basic needs are met.

At the end of his life, Maslow revisited his theory of human needs and realized there was a sixth need he hadn't considered in his model. He reasoned that after attainment of needs required for the self, the individual no longer focuses primarily on personal prosperity, but rather on the need for *transcendence*. At this level, an individual transcends limiting values, the self, the ego, and individual differences, accepts the natural world as it is, and wants to help the community. In other words, the peak of human motivation is *selflessness*.

OBJECTION 3: THERE ISN'T ENOUGH TO GO AROUND

The poor will always be with us—or so says the Bible. And in fact, many people want to make that argument: there just isn't enough to go around, someone will always be at the bottom of the ladder, someone will always get the short end of the stick. Let's test that supposition in a few arenas.

Housing. We've already discussed the rate of homelessness in the US as compared to the number of housing units sitting empty—for each of the more than half a million homeless persons in the US, there are almost two dozen empty properties. This misalignment of resources could be resolved if not for financial impediments.

Food. Globally, there are more than 800 million people experiencing hunger on a daily basis,[87] roughly 10 percent of the world population.[88] However, we have enough food production to feed 10 billion people, the population we are expected to reach in 2057[89]—we are simply not allocating it to people who need it. Furthermore, a recent study found that it was possible to feed that 10 billion *sustainably*.[90]

Wealth. We have all heard how 1 percent of the US population owns a large portion of the economic wealth, but do you know how immense this slice of the pie is? The Brookings Institution, a nonprofit public policy organization, conducted an in-depth study to better understand the inequality in the US and found that in 2016 the top income quintile (fifth) of the population held 77 percent of the total household wealth, while the entire middle class—the middle three income quintiles—held only 21 percent and the bottom quintile held a measly 2 percent.[91] Of the $98 trillion in wealth American households held, the top 1 percent *alone* owned over $25 trillion, while the entire middle class owned merely $18 trillion.

There is enough. There is enough housing to allow for safety and protection to all. There is enough food to feed and nourish everyone. There is enough wealth to grant comfort and dignity to every human being. We have *chosen* not to distribute our resources in a way that allows everyone a decent standard of living. In business they say that your spending demonstrates your priorities. We have simply not made it a priority to care for everyone.

OBJECTION 4: CAPITALISM WORKS BETTER THAN THIS WOULD

The old joke goes, "Capitalism is the worst economic system—except for all the others." I hope by this point you agree that the joke is wrong and that there are, indeed, better alternatives to capitalism. As we discussed extensively in the first part of the book, capitalism is wholly unsustainable due to its inherently competitive nature, which creates growth and inequality as a byproduct. Additionally, the profit motive incentivizes people to exploit natural resources and other people, which both create a degree of unsustainability, instability, and inequality within society.

The nature of the capitalist system itself promotes scarcity, exploitation, and division. The competitive, transaction-based system requires endless activity and disincentivizes the free and open sharing of goods and resources. While there may be some mechanism that would appear to make capitalism "work better," such as rules or regulations, closing tax loopholes, or just getting the right people into office, a capitalist society will never achieve anywhere close to the degree of sustainability or resource efficiency that is achievable in a moneyless society.

Furthermore, in our political system, neither the left nor the right possesses the power to enact the necessary measures to curtail the damage the capitalist system inflicts upon us and our environment. The real solutions are rarely mentioned as possibilities (they are rarely within the realm of thought, for that matter). So, we keep going back and forth between the right and left, from one ineffective solution to the next, all the while getting ever-more riled up at one another, with each side becoming increasingly convinced that the other side is the root of the problem, if not the root of all evil itself.

The reality, though, is that capitalism dooms both sides—dooms everyone—due to the structural constraints of the system itself. The only real, lasting solution is to completely reimagine, redesign, and overhaul the system from top to bottom. Only then will we possess the foundational infrastructure needed to implement better solutions free of the capitalist constraints that currently inhibit us from producing true abundance and prosperity for everyone.

OBJECTION 5: FREE MARKETS ARE THE SOLUTION

A *free market* is one in which buyers and sellers come together to exchange goods and services unrestricted by rules or regulations. Many Libertarians, Republicans, and conservatives argue that the market should, as much as possible, be left to its own devices without rules, regulations, or interventions to guide or correct it, and that the "invisible hand of the market"—that is, everyone acting in their own best interest—will somehow make everything work out better than if there were regulations or management of some sort.

First, truly free markets don't exist. There is always some sort of regulation, and different markets have differing levels of "freedom." The reason such regulation is needed is what we've been talking about throughout this whole book: the capitalist system favors competition over cooperation and incentivizes exploitation, manipulation, and hoarding.

Additionally, for a free market to be efficient, we need information symmetry. That is, both parties in a transaction need transparency and access to relevant information to make rational, informed decisions. Because of the profit incentive, business owners (and other players who benefit from the system) are incentivized to create barriers to transparency that hide information.

We see this lack of transparency when companies hide the damage in terms of their products' environmental or human costs. It manifests in things like the underpayment of women and Black, Indigenous, and People of Color (BIPOC). It leads to a US healthcare system that is so opaque it is not a functional market. It results in research findings that support the company funding the research, with unfavorable findings tucked away.

You can't have a system that encourages people to be selfish and expect to get generosity as a result. You can't design a system to run on competition and expect it to generate cooperation. You can't create a system that functions one way and expect it to produce results that run counter to that. The free market may be good for the GDP, but it's not good for people and the environment.

While we do want some elements of a "free" market, such as voluntary participation and lack of coercion, we don't want the profit system that incents people to "win" by cheating, acting unethically, hoarding, and exploiting people and natural resources.

OBJECTION 6: CRYPTOCURRENCIES ARE THE SOLUTION

Cryptocurrencies such as Bitcoin are digital mediums of exchange that work outside any central governmental or banking authority. Some people like to argue that cryptocurrencies will solve the problems that the market and government cannot by integrating new functions (such as contracts, regulations, or other incentives/disincentives) directly into the cryptocurrencies themselves.

These features most likely are a step in the right direction and may even have use during a transition to a moneyless society. However, the real problem with cryptocurrencies is that the market system and profit incentive still exist, which keeps the greater, activity-driven, exploitative system going in unsustainable perpetuity. In other words, cryptocurrency is just another form of money, and it will always produce the profit incentive since the use of money implies the use of a trade-based system.

As a not-insignificant sidenote, many cryptocurrencies currently require a significant amount of computing power, thus generating a large carbon footprint. While this drawback of cryptocurrencies can likely be mitigated, the market and profit systems themselves still remain.

OBJECTION 7: WE NEED THE PRICE MECHANISM

The price mechanism objection comes in the form of statements like "Centrally planned economic systems don't work" or "We need money to facilitate trade and distribution." In our modern economy, the price mechanism helps the market find equilibrium between supply and demand by serving as a sort of feedback tool that tells producers and suppliers how to distribute resources among competing interests.

The argument is that the absence of the price mechanism (or the presence of some central authority that attempts to control resources) would create distortions in the ability to allocate resources, and create problems when determining what to produce, how much, and where to send items. In other words, we would have chaos in production, which would lead to scarcity. Does this sound familiar? If so, it's because this is what the capitalist system inherently does, as we discussed in Chapter 1.

All the price mechanism does is tell us how much people are willing to pay in monetary form to gain access to particular resources. However, price has practically nothing to do with the resource's highest and best use, and often tells us little about the utility or ecological value of that item.

As discussed in Chapter 6 regarding the manufacturing of goods, we are technologically capable of using data gained directly from consumers to determine the details of demand and needed production. When people order goods or services online (or even take items off shelves at a store), data can go directly to automated production systems that calculate everything from how many of something to produce and where to send the items, to what types of materials are best suited for use in production. Peter Joseph elaborates on this subject in his talk, "Economic Calculation in a Natural Law/Resource-Based Economy":[92]

> The trick is to completely eliminate exchange and create a direct control and feedback link between the consumer and the means of production itself. The consumer becomes part of the means of production, and the "industrial complex," if you will, becomes nothing more than a tool that is accessed by the public to generate goods. In fact . . . the same system can be used for just about any societal calculation, virtually eliminating the state government, in fact, and politics as we know it. It is a participatory decision-making process.

In other words, not only can we replace everything the price mechanism does and do it more efficiently with our current state of technology, but we can also use that same technology to eliminate the vast majority of the workings and inefficiencies of the government as we know it, since the replacement system would provide a population with the collaborative tools to handle nearly any such decisions on their own. (For further information, also see the Society Library under the section on Governance and Decision-Making in Chapter 6.)

OBJECTION 8: THIS IS COMMUNISM & WON'T WORK

If you want to scare someone away from the ideas presented in this book, just shout "Communism!" or "Socialism!" These two terms have become bogey monsters in recent years, and this is probably the most common argument you will hear against a moneyless society. This objection also comes in the form of "Socialism/communism is evil and always results in [fill in the blank: corruption, authoritarianism, killing millions of people]."

Before addressing the objection, let's clarify the definition of these terms.

Socialism is a system in which the means of production are owned or controlled by the public/workers. The term can also refer to the distribution (or redistribution) of income/wealth more equitably throughout society. Generally, capitalism can exist alongside or in conjunction with socialist elements of the economy/government. Socialism is often considered to be a transitional period between capitalism and communism.

Communism is also a system in which the means of production are owned or controlled by the public or working class. Contemporary communism is often defined as the political philosophy that Marx described in the mid-1800s, which advocates the revolutionary overthrow of the wealthy, or "bourgeoisie," and the transfer of power to the working class, or "proletariat."

The tricky thing about defining communism and socialism, though, is that there are so many different definitions of the two terms and so many different branches and offshoots of each of them—all with their own nuances, theories, and trains of thought—that it's next to impossible to sort through them without studying the subject for years.

The reality is that there are certain parts of these concepts that apply to the models we are talking about in this book, and there are others that do not.

The parts that apply to the moneyless model we speak of are elimination of private property, shared ownership of the means of production, democratic/consensus decision-making, freedom of choice, and the other principles we discussed in Chapter 5.

The parts that do *not* apply are autocracy, control of the means of production by the state, coercion and killing to implement authoritarian policies, and other violent/revolutionary means of creating these systems.

Furthermore, the technological capabilities that existed in the times of Lenin, Stalin, Marx, et al. were nowhere near the capabilities that are in existence today. We can now automate a large portion of production and distribution—something that would have been impossible at the time of, say, the Bolshevik Revolution and formation of the USSR. We also have an unprecedented reason to create these systems and structures in the here and now—climate change and the fate of all the species on our planet. Moreover, we have a vastly greater understanding of our natural systems, how our world and universe operate, and how to harness these elements to our benefit.

Many supporters of a moneyless society say (emphatically) that they would like to leave all the "-isms" behind; they believe society is ready to embrace a new social and economic system that truly enables our full potential. Many state that this new and evolving economic model surpasses any ideologies of Marx or communism, since it considers and emphasizes modern developments such as the latest findings in science and technology, ecology, social sciences, and much more. Saying the systems and structures we describe is a type of communism would be akin to saying that the computer that I am typing this document on is a form of typewriter.

We know that when the types of systems we describe in this book have been attempted in the past, the results have often been promising, but they've also often been cut short or suppressed. This was the case with Project Cybersyn, a Chilean effort begun in 1971 and headed by renowned British theorist and cyberneticist Stafford Beer, which would have been the first and only cybernetically run socialist government system in the world, before or since. The project made innovative use of technology limited even for the time (using Telex machines, which were considered outdated at that point). It was a brief but dramatic experiment in which Chilean workers were given democratic and cooperative control of their factories. However, Chile's socialist president, Salvador Allende, died in the 1973 Nixon/CIA-backed coup, resulting in the placement of Augusto Pinochet, a brutal right-wing dictator, who remained in power for nearly two decades.

We also know that these types of systems we've been describing work in the present. At this writing, the Spanish village of Marinaleda, now run successfully by a far-left communist/socialist mayor for over thirty years, boasts a 2,500-person farming cooperative, no mortgages,[93] and no police force (saving them

$350,000 annually). Rojava, also known as the Autonomous Administration of North and East Syria (AANES), is a libertarian socialist region run under the principles of democratic confederalism (autonomous communities run cooperatively and democratically). Rojava challenges the wage/income model by bypassing it altogether and, in many cases, directly distributing produce and other necessities based on need instead. These successful communities are just a few examples of the systems and structures we may examine, duplicate, learn from, experiment with, and improve upon around the world in the years to come.

Whatever communities, systems, or designs we create, one thing is for certain: they will never have been tried before in exactly the way we're going to try them, and every community, cooperative, city, and region will have its own unique circumstances, cultures, quirks, and ways of doing things. The potential for variations on projects and experiments to adopt different methods and systems of governance and production is so vast that there is literally no limit to the combinations of technology, governing systems, environmental designs, and manufacturing we can try.

We could debate what to name each iteration of a moneyless society design, but the real goal is to achieve the outcome, not to write a dissertation about philosophical nuances. However, to reiterate—and this is crucial—if we are to successfully build a moneyless society, where people are free to do as they please and everyone is provided for, the entire system must be derived organically, voluntarily, and peacefully from the ground up. It cannot in any way involve top-down governmental mandates that force people into doing things they don't want to do, as we have sadly seen historically. Many people fail to recognize that a non-authoritarian version of these "socialized" systems is legitimately possible to construct and operate, but that was the impetus for this book—to illustrate that a nonauthoritarian type of cooperative society is possible and to outline how it could be achieved.

That's one of the main reasons why we promote the idea of universal basic goods and services—it's a self-explanatory term and goal in and of itself. People hear it and they can usually understand what it means the first time. And it describes what it is we want our systems and structures to do. At this point we need to worry less about names and instead focus on producing the outcomes we want.

Instead of asking "Is this socialism?" we can ask ourselves things like:

- "How can we use technology to make our environment and energy work for us?"
- "How can we foster cooperation and kindness within communities and among people from all walks of life?"
- "How can we create systems and structures that foster abundance and restore our environment?"
- "How can we create a better world, that we all want to live and participate in, and that can be sustained for many generations to come?"

Those aren't easy questions, and I don't have all the answers. I do, however, have a few solid directions we can go from here. In the last chapter, we'll take a brief look at what steps we can take in our lives, today, to start to create this change.

CHAPTER 9

A CALL TO ACTION

We have the most significant work that humanity has ever had, with the most significant capabilities, which also means the most potential to impact the biggest picture that any humans have ever had.

DANIEL SCHMACHTENBERGER, FOUNDING MEMBER,
THE CONSILIENCE PROJECT

Welcome to the last chapter of the book. If you are overwhelmed with all the information we have covered and want to do something but aren't sure where to start, I have some good news for you—you are not alone. Plenty of people would like to help solve our society's biggest problems but aren't sure what actions are the most impactful. This chapter is here to help you start taking steps, making changes, and incorporating these principles into your life so you *can* make an impact.

Fortunately, there are probably more ways to help than you realize. In fact, there are so many things you could do that deciding what to do can be overwhelming. We can all change *many* things in our lives to help our society grow in a more positive direction; however, we have only so many hours in a day, and using our time wisely is important if we are to make any substantial progress.

To help in that regard, what follows are five key categories of things you may be able to do in your community. If enough of us start taking actions, both big and small, it will noticeably move the needle in the direction of a better world.

ACTION 1. TALK ABOUT MONEYLESS SOCIETY IDEAS

The idea of a moneyless society in some ways seems fantastical, and indeed it will take a long, gradual process to create one. Part of that process is simply talking about the possibility in a way that it becomes part of the mainstream conversation—that it seems less fantastical and more possible.

The *Overton window*, also known as *the window of discourse*, is defined as the range of political ideas that are reasonably acceptable in the public's point of view at a certain point in time. What is or is not considered "acceptable" is rarely stated explicitly; however, the limits of the Overton window are understood when a point of view or suggestion is ridiculed or dismissed without a properly objective examination. Politicians are often skilled at detecting the limits of the Overton window and designing policies that push those limits in the direction they see as most beneficial for the general populace. For example, over the past few years Bernie Sanders's idea of Medicare for All has moved from outside the Overton window into the realm of reasonable discussion.

The idea of communism as a political and economic foundation in the United States of America is completely outside the Overton window to most individuals today. To even suggest that communism could or should be implemented would be considered absurd (if not outright harmful to your health) in many public political conversations. This is not so much the case in many places in Europe. In the UK, Jeremy Corbyn, former leader of the Labour party (2015–2020), which is the main opposition to the Conservative party, is a self-proclaimed socialist. And while Corbyn leans more toward the center-left than a communist would, in the UK, conversations about communism, socialism, and "leftism" in general are far more common, far more informed, and much less taboo than in the United States.

It is often this truncated range of "acceptable" discourse that keeps society trapped in its current state. All too often we hold back our true thoughts or perspectives, simply due to fear of what other people will think. This is understandable, because our society generally rewards those who reinforce "acceptable" ideas and punishes those who are furthest outside the boundaries. (Notice the feedback loop.)

However, the more we bring seemingly "extreme" ideas into the light and discuss them as politically and socially viable options, the more we can shift the paradigm. As journalist Caitlin Johnstone elaborates in her article "The Incredible Shrinking Overton Window":[94]

> The plutocrat-owned narrative managers of the political/ media class work constantly to shrink the Overton window, the spectrum of debate that is considered socially acceptable. They do this by framing more and more debates in terms of *how* the oligarchic empire should be sustained and supported, steering them away from debates about *whether* that empire should be permitted to exist at all.
>
> They get people debating whether there should be some moderate changes made or no meaningful changes at all, rather than the massive, sweeping changes we all know need to be made to the entire system. . . .

They get people debating whether Bernie Sanders is electable or too radical, rather than discussing what it says about the status quo that his extremely modest proposals which every other major country already implements are treated as something outlandish in the United States. . . .

They get people debating whether Fox or MSNBC is the real "fake news," rather than whether the entirety of mainstream media is oligarchic propaganda. . . .

They get people debating what should be done with money, not whether the concept of money itself is in need of a complete overhaul.

To make change and act in accordance with what is best for humanity and the planet, it's our responsibility to educate ourselves about these subjects, to talk about them with our family, friends, neighbors, and coworkers, and to bring awareness to the possibilities we describe in this book. It is up to us to bring up terminology like a "moneyless society," a "resource-based economy," or even "techno-libertarian eco-socialism," and help people understand what those terms mean, how the concepts could potentially work, and why they are important to learn about. It is of benefit to talk about the problems with profit and the monetary system; about the benefits that can be realized if we pursue the principles in this book; about climate change and the limited amount of time we have on this planet to start acting in accord with the principles of sustainability, and the consequences if we do not. This discourse helps expand people's awareness, and helps bring these topics into more acceptance, so that we can begin to bring a new way of life into existence in our world.

The Overton window can be moved, and it can be moved quickly, especially in times of crisis or great upheaval. Coming back to systems thinking, a large shift in the Overton window usually means that something has affected one of the highest leverage points for influencing change in a population. If our society can become more educated and informed about the crisis at hand, about the urgency and seriousness of the matter, and the ultimate cause of it—the monetary system and the inherent growth required to sustain it—then we can use the leverage point of changing our collective paradigm from one that needs competition and growth to one that focuses on cooperation and regeneration. We would be able to change our purpose from success, winning, and accumulation to prosperity, harmony, and abundance. These are the conversations that need to become acceptable in public discourse for us to have a chance at influencing real change.

ACTION 2. GET THIS INFORMATION INTO THE WORLD

As hard as many of us work to get the moneyless society message out there, when we talk to people in public, it seems few have heard of these concepts. To effect real change, this information needs to be blasted from here to outer space and everywhere in between.

You can help by doing what you can to get the word out there. Write a blog post about the subject, or submit an article to be considered as a guest author on MoneylessSociety.com. Check out our Moneyless Society Facebook page and group and share some of the content. Listen to our podcast, become educated about the subject, and help spread the word. Post TikTok videos or tell your friends about these ideas while having a few beers on a Friday night. Or contribute to existing organizations working toward these goals. In addition to the list in Appendix

A, we also have an online list of resources posted on our website at MoneylessSociety.com/resources.

Consider buying a copy or two of this book for other people in your life, such as friends, family, your boss, coworkers, teachers, your hairstylist, your congressperson, your neighbors. Leaving a good review for us on Amazon or Google always helps too. As these concepts become more widespread and enough people are on board with building a better system, collectively we can take larger-scale action and create the communities, systems, and organizations we want.

As a note, people often think it is ironic or hypocritical for an organization called "Moneyless Society" to be generating money through sales and actively asking for donations. However, the only way we can build the systems and structures we advocate in this book is through using the structures we currently have at our disposal. For now, this unavoidably includes the use of money to purchase assets and pay people. The resources and machinery needed to develop new structures still cost money, and people still need money to survive. There is no easy way around this. It is only through the intentional creation of business structures that can design, build, and operate the systems needed to provide universal basic goods and services that we can adopt the type of socioeconomic system that we advocate in this book. And, as much as some people will not want to hear it, that will take raising both awareness and money.

ACTION 3. HELP AN EXISTING ORGANIZATION OR CREATE YOUR OWN

Plenty of organizations working toward a better world can use help. The Venus Project, The Zeitgeist Movement, One Community Global, and many others that you can find in Appendix A are looking for volunteers and provide numerous ways in which you can contribute.

Our organization, Moneyless Society, has numerous tasks ready to be assigned in a variety of areas: our podcast, website, and social media channels; a YouTube channel and a film; a regenerative farm and biochar project; and several other projects on deck. If you are interested in helping us achieve the goals we talk about in this book or would like more information, please send us an email at contact@MoneylessSociety.com. Donations are also welcome, and more information can be provided upon request. Check our website for regular updates on our projects.

Additionally, if you see a problem that is not being addressed or you possess a skill that could be of benefit to the community, maybe it is time to start your own business or organization. If you're not in the position to start a full-fledged cooperative, consider forming a business with the intent of converting it to a cooperative in the future. The greater the number of established organizations we get operating on the same page and cooperating with one another, the better. And if you want to discuss how to incorporate the ideas in this book, please contact us to set up a conversation.

ACTION 4. DEVELOP NEW SKILLS

To build the systems of the future, we need more people with STEM-related skills—that is, science, technology, engineering, and math. This includes disciplines such as robotics, automation, computer science, systems analysis, automated data acquisition, nanotechnology, biotechnology, chemistry, botany, oceanography, ecology, sociology, psychology, behavioral sciences, artificial intelligence, industrial design, sustainability, soil science, agroecology, nutrition, medicine, architecture, 3D prototyping, and much, much more. If you are looking for an interesting, rewarding field, there is no lack of choice.

For many people, learning how to better communicate and cooperate with others will be an invaluable skill in the future. On-line courses abound for learning things like consensus decision-making, effective listening/communication techniques, mindfulness, leadership, teamwork, negotiation (yes, negotiation will exist in the absence of money), and more. Additionally, the possibilities for self-education at little or no expense are greater today than they have ever been. Thanks to the internet, instruction and learning have opened their doors beyond the schoolhouse, beyond the university, with many high-quality courses and online collaborative learning spaces for both children and adults. If you are interested in exploring some of the many free and low-cost educational options available online today, One Community Global has compiled an extensive list at onecommunityglobal.org/free-education-resources.

ACTION 5. FIND & USE EXISTING RESOURCES & STRANDED ASSETS

You know that empty field down at the end of the street? Or that abandoned building a few blocks away? Often those are valuable assets, just sitting there unused, that can be repurposed and retrofitted for many of the plans and projects described in this book. Even a small plot of land in your neighborhood can be a good place to start a collaborative project. Talk to property owners and see if you can work out a deal to use their land for innovative projects that help create community resilience and social justice.

Consider projects involving regenerative agriculture, aquaponics, desert-greening, community composting centers, water collection, educational facilities, "makerspaces," workspaces, tool libraries, or cooperative businesses. The more people can work together, share available resources, and build systems that provide resilience, redundancy, decentralization, and systemic reciprocity, the greater and faster the shift will be toward a moneyless society and the obsolescence of capitalism.

It is unlikely that a moneyless society will simply come about without a focused intention to create it, and it's also unlikely that a complete overhaul of our socioeconomic system will happen anytime soon. It is more likely that the beginnings of a transition to a moneyless society will appear in an organic, local manner and will consist of smaller changes that communities and individuals take to eliminate their dependence on standard corporate production and the financial system. It's through these smaller changes that the gradual elimination of unnecessary jobs—and eventually entire industries—will begin to take shape in a transition to more sustainable, efficient ways of life.

As individuals and as a society, we must develop the skills and habits that can take us toward a moneyless society and begin to implement them in our daily lives. Only as people see and experience firsthand what we are capable of will they come to realize what is possible, and only then will more demand for such systems be created. To effect change, we must be the change. The process of building the change we seek is the solution to the problem. As Marcus Aurelius said, "The impediment to action advances action. What stands in the way becomes the way."

We're at the point right now where we can continue upholding the status quo, or we can come together and head in a different direction. For people who aren't exposed to the harsh reality that our economic system creates daily, it's easy to ignore the warning signs and carry on with routine. But for those of us keenly aware of the circumstances we face, going about life with our head in the sand feels like a violation of our integrity, and rightly so. Those of us who can wait no longer know who we are. If we want to change the world, we must work to build the change we want to see. And that work begins now.

ACKNOWLEDGMENTS

There is no way I could have written this book alone. The only reason it has come to fruition is because of the efforts of countless people—many of whom came long before me—and decades of collective work. Among the people who have contributed to the information/efforts herein and were necessary to put this book together in its current form, I would like to thank:

Karin Wiberg (pronounced CAR-in) and her team at Clear Sight Books (an appropriate name for working on this topic), for taking my initial rant and, over the course of two and a half years, turning it into a real, solid book. Working with you has been an expert education in writing and communication (my own personal composition class!). I hope to work with you on many more projects in the years to come.

Amanda Smith, for being the first person to really come on board 100 percent with the Moneyless Society organization, for handling the vast majority of operations and enabling me to write this book, and for doing so much every day to keep this all moving forward. Additionally, your insights and critiques for this book have been invaluable. Your efforts are noticed and appreciated.

Zachary Marlow, for many valuable insights regarding this book, and for being a good friend who consistently expands my awareness and horizons. You are a masterful communicator and a production wizard. It is only a matter of time before your talent and dedication propel your creative genius into the spotlight.

Brenda Damasceno, for assisting in countless hours of research, offering many valuable insights, and being open-minded and receptive to these ideas. You made a substantial contribution to this work, and I wish you the absolute best on all your future endeavors.

The many thinkers, teachers, and supporters I've learned from, been inspired by, and/or worked with (in no particular order): Jacque Fresco, Roxanne Meadows, Peter Joseph, Jae Sabol, Colin Turner, Chris Agnos, R. Buckminster Fuller, Noam Chomsky, David Graeber, Yanis Varoufakis, Slavoj Žižek, Ash Sarkar, Abby Martin, Lee Camp, Bhaskar Sunkara, Daniel Christian Wahl, Daniel Pinchbeck, Richard D. Wolff, Rutger Bregman, David Peter Stroh, Umair Haque, Travis Grant, Elizabeth Reizinger, Robert Shields, Arjang Jameh, Alex W. Fink, Lavra Tamutus, Sunni Yen, John Yen, Tomas Cook, David Smith, Thomas Wright, Michael Plischke, Allan Chornak, Kai Jeremy, Liam Keegan, JT Walgren, Aboubakre Harakat, Ananda Reeves, James Ehrlich, Chris McManus, Quae Frei, Troy Wiley, Vladimir Alzamora Guzman, Julie Glasscock, Helena Norberg-Hodge, Rod Keays, Robert Schram, Phillip Gilbert, John Perkins, Professor James Gilligan, "Rosie & JJ," Nathan Jones, Daniel ("Anark") Baryon, Jeff Cates, MA, Ronald Wolfe, Nikhil Kulkarni, Lorenzo ("Mr. Kill Money") Segarra II, Josie Loner, Aaron Frost, Alexander Nemo, Alex Atuheire, Patrick Conlon, Vincent Ballerz, Zak Jennings, Prentice Reid, "Comrade Joey," Carlos Plazola, Larry Norris, PhD, Katherine Marsden, Daan Gorter, Steven D. Grumbine, Ayman Ahmed, David Busch-Lilly, Yavor Tarinski, "Flower Garden," and "Wild Quetzal."

All our past, present, and future volunteers, as well as all the collaborators and guests who have come on our podcast (and who have yet to come on). Thank you for the work you have done and continue to do. We are a team working toward the same goal, and without all of you, this work would not be possible. You are an inspiration to me, and I consider you my extended family.

Our many followers and supporters, for listening to us and for believing in us and the vision we hold. Let's build the change we wish to see—together—one day and one step at a time. We're just getting started, and I'm looking forward to the incredible journey ahead with all of you.

And now—onward and upward!

RESOURCES

This appendix lists organizations, movements, and resources that may be of interest in understanding how we create a more sustainable society. As time goes on, some organizations may change their names, values, or goals, or cease to exist altogether. I would simply like to recognize and give credit to these organizations for their contributions toward sustainability and making the world a better place for us all.

Disclaimer: Just because an organization or community is listed does not mean it agrees with or supports any or all of the ideas in this book; nor does it mean it is associated with me or with other organizations listed. I have shared limited information about each; to learn more, please visit their respective websites and materials.

Arcosanti (arcosanti.org). Community in Arizona that uses "arcology"—a combination of architecture and ecology—to offer an alternative to urban sprawl.

The Auravana Project (auravana.org). Organization developing and detailing systems, structures, and standards for a highly automated, regenerative, community-oriented, moneyless society.

Auroville (auroville.org). Spiritual evolutionary community founded in 1968 with over 3,300 residents from sixty countries. Based on human unity, integral yoga, and experimentation in all fields, Auroville addresses healthcare, architecture, the environment, and more.

Blue Frontiers (bluefront.org). Organization developing sustainable floating islands with unique governing frameworks.

Buckminster Fuller Institute (bfi.org). Organization that develops programs to deploy strategies that radically regenerate Earth's ecosystems through a focus on systems change.

Circle Economy (circle-economy.com). Circular solutions for businesses and cities.

Communiivate (communiivate.com). A social network with features to connect like-minded change-makers and promote collaboration.

The Commons Transition Primer (primer. commonstransition.org). Policy proposals and ideas to implement a Social Knowledge Economy for "sharing what's abundant, and protecting what's scarce."

Damanhur (damanhur.org). Multilingual, spiritual "laboratory" community in Italy.

The Earth Charter (earthcharter.org). Document with sixteen principles for sustainability; also an education center that supports the movement.

Earthship Biotecture (earthshipglobal.com). Company for artistic eco-construction and self-sufficient living.

Fab City Project (fab.city). Initiative to have cities create everything they consume by 2054.

Fab Foundation (fabfoundation.org). Foundation that facilitates the international Fab Lab Network.

Fab Labs (fablabs.io). Network of over 1,800 digital fabrication laboratories around the world.

Farm Bot (farm.bot). Home-based, open-source, CNC-automated agriculture machine.

Federation of Egalitarian Communities (thefec.org). Union of egalitarian communities.

Foundation for Intentional Community (ic.org). International directory of intentional communities, with additional resources.

Gaianet (gaianet.earth). Collective of mission-aligned projects and professionals with a shared vision of a New Earth, rooted in love and harmony with abundance for all.

Global Ecovillage Network (ecovillage.org). International directory of ecovillages, with additional resources.

Kadagaya (kadagaya.org). Research center and experimental village in Peru.

Kiss the Ground (kisstheground.com). Movement dedicated to spreading awareness about regenerative agriculture.

Lammas Ecovillage (lammas.org.uk). Community in the UK pioneering sustainable living.

Libcom.org (libcom.org). Website about libertarian communism.

Magnova (magnova.space). An online hub for facilitating direct action, organization, and problem-solving.

MIT Open Agriculture Initiative (media.mit.edu/groups/open-agriculture-openag/). Initiative that built open resources to enable a global community to accelerate digital agricultural innovation; website contains information about past research.

Money Free Party (moneyfreeparty.org.nz). Political party that promotes the ideas and concepts of a moneyless society or resource-based economy.

New Economy Coalition (neweconomy.net). Network of organizations building a future where people, community, and ecosystems thrive.

On the Commons (onthecommons.org). Commons movement strategy center and magazine.

One Community Global (onecommunityglobal.org).

Organization creating open-source resources and solutions for all aspects of sustainable living.

Open Access Economy (openaccesseconomy.org). Wiki for creating proposed alternative method of organizing human society without the limitations of trade and markets.

Open Knowledge Foundation (okfn.org). Organization creating and driving forward open knowledge and open data around the world.

Open Source Ecology (opensourceecology.org). Organization developing open-source industrial machines.

P2P Foundation (wiki.p2pfoundation.net). Organization/ network dedicated to advocacy and research of commons-oriented peer-to-peer (P2P) dynamics in society.

People & Planet (peopleandplanet.org). Student network in UK for social and environmental justice.

Precious Plastic (preciousplastic.com). Alternative open-source recycling system run by people around the world.

ReGen Villages (regenvillages.com). Technology-enabled, bio-regenerative, and resilient communities, with critical life support systems of food, water, energy, and circular waste/resource management at the neighborhood scale.

The Seasteading Institute (seasteading.org). Nonprofit think tank promoting the creation of floating ocean cities as a solution to some of the world's most pressing problems, such as rising sea levels, overpopulation, and poor governance.

Sharebay (sharebay.org). Global online network for free sharing of goods and services.

The Society Library (societylibrary.org). Organization dedicated to archiving ideas, ideologies, and worldviews to create a fully intentional, collaborative humanity that maximizes freedom through access to information.

Solidarity Economy (solidarityeconomics.org).
Collaboration using data and analysis to contribute to a
more powerful, well-resourced, intersectional, and
intersectoral movement for equity.

The Story of Stuff Project (storyofstuff.org). Organization
whose mission is to transform the way we make, use, and
throw away "stuff" so that it is healthy, sustainable, and fair.

Sustainable Human (sustainablehuman.org). Nonprofit
that creates educational and inspiring video stories that
evolve human consciousness by addressing the roots of our
many sustainability crises.

The Systems Thinker (thesystemsthinker.com). Website for
thinking in terms of systems theory.

Tamera (tamera.org). Organization developing Healing
Biotopes—decentralized, autonomous community models—
as a foundation for a culture free of fear and violence.

Technocracy (technocracyinc.org). Organization that
advocates scientifically objective functional decision-
making to mitigate harmful effects on humans and the
environment.

Transition Network (transitionnetwork.org). A movement
of communities coming together to reimagine and rebuild
our world.

Transition US (transitionus.org). Large grassroots
organization and network seeking to build community
resilience; US hub of the Transition Network.

TROM (tromsite.com). Organization and educational project
that showcases how trade creates most of the world's
problems and advocates social change.

The Venus Project (thevenusproject.com). Organization
that proposes a holistic approach called a resource-based
economy, utilizing the most current technological and

scientific advances to provide the highest possible living standard for all people on Earth.

World Socialist Movement (worldsocialism.org). International organization of socialist parties.

The Zeitgeist Movement (thezeitgeistmovement.com). Global grassroots movement with chapters in over seventy countries; advocates transitioning to a resource-based economy and, like The Venus Project, recommends implementation of sustainable ecology and the scientific administration of society.

GLOSSARY

Agroecology. An approach to agriculture that takes into account the entire ecosystem and impacts on it. It includes numerous methodologies and techniques, such as soil/environmental regeneration, holistic grazing practices, silvopasture, desert-greening, carbon farming/sequestration, and permaculture; it also entails a focus on specific cultures and how they relate to food and agriculture, and how soil health and agricultural practices affect the nutritional qualities of foods. See also *regenerative agriculture*.

Analysis. The taking apart of something to understand the pieces. Compare to *synthesis* and *emergence*.

Anarcho-Syndicalism. Philosophy that views labor unions and the syndication of workers as a tactic for gaining control and influence in a capitalist society and as a catalyst for social change.

Antifragility. A concept coined by Nicolas Taleb in his 2008 book of the same name; describes a property of systems that enables them to adapt and become more resilient when confronted with adversity, shock, or disorder.

Archetype. A commonly existing pattern in *systems thinking*. See also *conflicting goals*, *fixes that fail*, *success to the successful*, and *tragedy of the commons*.

Artificial Scarcity. When things are purposely withheld or restricted for use so they can be sold for profit. Compare to *chaotic scarcity*.

Balancing Feedback Loop. When the outcome of a certain action is one that keeps bringing something back to a certain level or equilibrium; also called *negative feedback loop*. Compare to *reinforcing feedback loop*.

BIPOC. Acronym for Black, Indigenous, and People of Color.

Capitalism. A socioeconomic system whereby the means of production are held by private interests (as opposed to the state, the public, or the workers) and controlled for the purpose of generating profit and wealth for those private interests. Compare to *communism* and *socialism*.

Cascade (Cascading) Effects. Outcomes or events that occur in a chain, with one occurrence affecting something else, which in turn affects something else, and so on and so forth; a chain reaction.

Causality. The recognition and relationship of cause and effect.

Chaotic Production. Production systems that lack proper accountability, communication, or management protocols with respect to manufacturing requirements, consumer demand, distribution systems, or externalities regarding resources, human, or environmental effects.

Chaotic Scarcity. A lack of items or services created as an unintentional side effect of manufacturing, production, and distribution being managed in a disconnected, unorganized, and chaotic manner. Compare to *artificial scarcity*.

Circular Economy. See *closed-loop economy*.

Climate Change. A change in the average weather patterns of a region over time, including warming temperatures, increased or decreased rainfall, and more frequent extreme weather.

Closed-Loop Economy. An economic system by which all

"waste" outputs are utilized as inputs for other purposes; recycling, reusing, upgrading, upcycling, repurposing, and retrofitting are all techniques that help achieve this goal. Also called *circular economy*.

Co-op. See *cooperative*.

Commodification. The process by which most everyday goods, services, and necessities have been turned into commodities that can be procured only through purchase.

Commodity. Any "product" that is created primarily for sale on the open market, or anything that is regularly bought or sold.

Commons. Land or other property that is held in common, usually equally, by a group or community.

Communism. A political and economic system in which the means of production are owned or controlled by the public or working class. Contemporary communism is often defined as the political philosophy that Marx described in the mid-1800s, which advocates the revolutionary overthrow of the wealthy, or "bourgeoisie," and the transfer of power to the working class, or "proletariat." Compare to *capitalism* and *socialism*.

Conflicting Goals. An archetype in systems thinking that occurs when the pursuit of two goals at odds with one another results in decisions that contribute to the success of one goal to the detriment of the other. See also *fixes that fail*, *success to the successful*, and *tragedy of the commons*.

Cooperative. A legal and business structure that codifies equitable/equal ownership and democratic decision-making structures into accessible, practical business practices. Also called *co-op*.

Counterintuitive Results. Expecting one outcome and getting the opposite; unexpected results.

Degrowth. See *post growth*.

Derivatives. Financial instruments that are essentially bets or contracts based on various types of underlying financial assets.

Dystopia. A society in which people lead wretched, dehumanized, fearful lives. Compare to *protopia* and *utopia*.

Ecological Balance. A broad principle that encompasses the myriad relationships between our environment, the biosphere, and our socioeconomic system, and involves the sustainable management and regeneration of resources, along with other interactions with and investments in our biosphere.

Ecological Impact. The effect an action or cause has on the environment; for example, pollution as a result of product manufacturing or the clearing of forests for agricultural purposes.

Ecological Value. The value something (such as a tree, lake, or insect) holds with respect to being part of the natural environment. Compare to *exchange value* and *use value*.

Emergence. The outcome of synergy, the process of things coming together in a self-organizing way and forming something new that takes on properties not found in any of its constituent parts. Compare to *analysis* and *synthesis*.

Enclosure Acts. Specific laws related to *enclosures*.

Enclosures. A period or process by which commonly held land was fenced in and enclosed in England and then other parts of the world. Facilitated and enforced by the *Enclosure Acts*.

Equality. In the context of this book, refers to the distribution of resources or responsibilities evenly, regardless of past or current circumstances or inequities. Compare to *equity*, *inequality*, and *social justice*.

Equity. In the context of this book, refers to the distribution of resources in a manner that reflects past inequities or inequalities, so the outcome is fairer though it often leaves the system that created the dysfunction intact. Compare to *equality*, *inequality*, and *social justice*.

Exchange Value. The value of a commodity when it is traded, or the price of an item when it is bought or sold; the price a buyer is willing to pay and a seller is willing to sell an item for on an open market. Compare to *ecological value* and *use value*.

Exploitation. Refers to the use of a person, place, resource, animal, or other thing for some sort of benefit; can refer to the general use of something for a purpose, or in the capitalist system, it mainly refers to people or things being employed or used in the pursuit of profit.

Externalities. Side effects or consequences of the extraction of resources or manufacturing and distribution of items, or other effects of the capitalist system that are not reflected in the price of an item or service.

Feedback Loop. The sequence in a cause-and-effect relationship where the output of the process is returned as an input. See also *balancing feedback loop* and *reinforcing feedback loop*.

Fiat Currency. A currency that is not fixed in value; a currency whose value can increase or decrease relative to commodities or other currencies.

Fixes That Fail. An archetype in systems thinking whereby the short-term solution to a problem inadvertently causes the original problem to become worse in the long term. See also *conflicting goals*, *success to the successful*, and *tragedy of the commons*.

Flow. In systems thinking, the rate at which a stock builds and/or depletes. Compare to *stock*.

Highest Good of All. The idea of acting in a manner that is in the best interest of everyone; common-sense approach that advocates empathy, communication, transparency, and working through differences to create positive transformation for all life on Earth, with the overarching theme of stewardship for one another and the environment.

Hoarding. Accumulating or storing more than one needs.

Inequality. In the context of this book, refers to the unevenness of wealth/resource distribution and the disparity of opportunities and conditions in and between groups of people and regions around the world. Compare to *equality*, *equity*, and *social justice*.

Interconnectedness. A principle that states that everything affects everything else to some degree, however small.

Internet of Things (IoT). A network that enables sensors and devices to communicate with each other.

Interoperability. The ability of items or technologies to work with one another in compatible ways.

Leverage Points. Specific places or areas of focus where we can make changes in systems that will influence the outcome in different ways; stronger leverage points allow changes to be made more easily.

Localization. The practice of deriving resources and manufacturing goods and services as close to the end user as possible to eliminate unnecessary travel and waste.

Means of Production. Property, machines, land, factories, buildings, intellectual property, and so on that are used to manufacture and deliver products and services.

Modularity. The ability to put things together or take them apart in standardized pieces.

Negative Feedback Loop. See *balancing feedback loop*.

Open Source. Refers to information, designs, software, data, and digital or other property that is freely accessible, viewable, or editable by the public; public information, often held without copyrights or patents.

Operant Conditioning. A learning process by which humans and animals behave in such a way as to obtain rewards and avoid punishments; the paradigm or study of such. See also *positive reinforcement*.

Overton Window. The range of political or social ideas that are reasonably acceptable in the public's point of view at a given point in time. Also called the *window of discourse*.

Personal Property. Items that are designated and designed for one's own use, such as one's clothing, furniture, residence, or other personal possessions. Compare to *private property*, *public property*, and *real property*.

Planned Obsolescence. The intentional future nonfunctionality of goods due to lack of replacement parts, noncompatibility with upgrades or new technology, or the use of less-than-optimal designs or materials.

Positive Feedback Loop. See *reinforcing feedback loop*.

Positive Reinforcement. A principle that means people or animals are more likely to continue doing things for which they are rewarded; rewarding people or animals for performing the desired behavior. See also *operant conditioning*.

Post Growth. A phase or era of controlled economic contraction intended to curtail much of the unnecessary activity generated by the capitalist market system, thereby more effectively addressing resource overshoot and climate change; also called *degrowth*.

Post-Scarcity Economy. A society or economy in which there is no longer a need for money or profit because necessities (and "luxuries") are abundant and provided to everyone for free through automation and environmentally friendly regenerative systems and technologies. Also called *post-scarcity society*.

Post-Scarcity Society. See *post-scarcity economy*.

Private Property. In the context of this book, private property refers to property that is owned or controlled by private interests for the purpose of obtaining profits on a commercial basis. Compare to *personal property*, *public property*, and *real property*.

Profit. Any excess money or wealth that a company, person, or institution procures through the course of business and is left after all expenses are paid.

Protopia. A society that moves in a positive direction by functioning with balance and synergy; in opposition to the idea of *dystopia*; a realistic alternative to the concept of a *utopia*.

Public Property. Property that is owned or controlled by the government or public in general. Compare to *personal property*, *private property*, and *real property*.

Real Property. Property that is immovable, such as land, buildings, and factories. Compare to *personal property*, *private property*, and *public property*.

Regenerative Agriculture. A type of agriculture that focuses on restoring soil health, sequestering carbon, healing the environment, increasing biodiversity, and fighting climate change through a variety of natural, technological, and restorative practices. See also *agroecology*.

Reinforcing Feedback Loop. When the outcome of a certain action perpetuates conditions that produce more of the same result, creating a self-reinforcing loop of cause and effect; also called a *positive feedback loop*. Compare to *balancing feedback loop*.

Resource Overshoot. An amount of environmental impact or consumption that pushes a natural system past the point of sustainability; includes overextraction of resources as well as putting too much waste into the environment.

Sharing Economy. An economy or society wherein many goods and services are shared or provided on an as-needed basis; an access-based economy rather than ownership-based economy.

Silvopasture. The practice of integrating trees and foraging livestock on the same land.

Social Justice. The fair treatment of all people, including those who have been marginalized or mistreated in the past; the fundamental restructuring of systems to repair dysfunctional relationships and outcomes within the economy and society so that all have equal access to resources and opportunities in the future. Compare to *equality*, *equity*, and *inequality*.

Socialism. A political and economic system in which the means of production are owned or controlled by the public/workers. The term can also refer to the distribution (or redistribution) of income/wealth more equitably throughout society. Compare to *capitalism* and *communism*.

Sociocracy. A governance model that emphasizes the creation of psychologically safe environments and productive organizations; focuses on the use of consent and decision-making by people who have shared goals or work processes.

Stock. In systems thinking, how much of something there is in some definable measure, or how much has built up over time. Compare to *flow*.

Stranded Asset. An asset, such as a building or equipment, that no longer provides an economic return based on its original intent.

Success to the Successful. An archetype in systems thinking that means when one is already successful, it becomes easier to gain more success. See also *conflicting goals*, *fixes that fail*, and *tragedy of the commons*.

Surplus. The amount of something that is left after needs have been satisfied; for example, what is left over from a harvest after storing enough food for one's family and enough seeds for the next crop.

Surplus Value. The excess value (monetary or otherwise) that is extracted by the owners of the means of production after the workers are paid.

Synthesis. The combination of multiple elements to create something new; the act of understanding the whole and recognizing how individual elements relate to and interact with one another. Compare to *analysis* and *emergence*.

Systemic Reciprocity. When items and necessities are provided through voluntary participation in an economic system without the necessity for trade or transactions; the reciprocal system proposed in this book eliminates unnecessary human labor and provides an abundance of goods and services through cooperation, technology, and ecological stewardship in return for voluntary contributions. Compare to *transactional reciprocity*.

Systems Theory. See *systems thinking*.

Systems Thinking. A methodological approach to analysis and problem solving that examines the causes, effects, relationships, and feedback loops between different elements in our world, and how they interact and compound with one another over time to produce various results. Also called *systems theory*.

Tragedy of the Commons. An archetype in systems thinking that occurs when individuals act in their own interest and, as a result, collectively the population causes damage to or plunders a common resource. See also *conflicting goals*, *fixes that fail*, and *success to the successful*.

Trade-Based Reciprocity. See *transactional reciprocity*.

Transactional Reciprocity. When items and necessities are procured through trade or transactions. Also called *trade-based reciprocity*. Compare to *systemic reciprocity*.

Universal Basic Goods and Services (UBGS) System. A system designed to provide the general public with all goods and services deemed necessary for everyday operation in society. Compare to *universal basic income system*.

Universal Basic Income (UBI) System. A system in which people receive money to purchase basic goods and services. Compare to *universal basic goods and services system*.

Use Value. An item's use, or what it can be used for. Also called *utility*. Compare to *exchange value* and *ecological value*.

Utility. See *use value*.

Utopia. A place of perfection, especially regarding laws, governance, and social conditions. Compare to *dystopia* and *protopia*.

Window of Discourse. See *Overton window*.

NOTES

[1] "Stats and Events," California Department of Forestry and Fire Protection (CAL FIRE), accessed 18 February 2022 (https://www.fire.ca.gov/stats-events/).

[2] A.B.A. Slangen, M. Carson, C.A. Katsman, R.S.W. van de Wal, A. Köhl, L.L. A Vermeersen, and D. Stammer, "Projecting twenty-first century regional sea-level changes," *Climatic Change* 124 (18 March 2014).

[3] "Great Barrier Reef has lost half of its corals since 1995," *BBC News*, 14 October 2020 (https://www.bbc.com/news/world-australia-54533971).

[4] "What is the sixth mass extinction and what can we do about it?" World Wildlife Fund, Inc., 2022 March 15 (https://www.worldwildlife.org/stories/what-is-the-sixth-mass-extinction-and-what-can-we-do-about-it).

[5] "Ten richest men double their fortunes in pandemic while incomes of 99 percent of humanity fall," Oxfam International, 17 January 2022 (https://www.oxfam.org/en/press-releases/ten-richest-men-double-their-fortunes-pandemic-while-incomes-99-percent-humanity).

[6] Peter Joseph, director and writer, *Zeitgeist: Addendum* (film), United States, Gentle Machine Productions, 2008.

[7] Sonia Harmand, Jason E. Lewis, Craig S. Feibel, Christopher J. Lepre, Sandrine Prat, Arnaud Lenoble, Xavier Boës, et al., "3.3-million-year-old stone tools from Lomekwi 3, West Turkana, Kenya," *Nature* 521, no. 7552 (2015).

[8] Alina Polianskaya, "Humans may have been trading with each other as far back as 300,000 years," *Inews.co.uk*, 15 March 2018 (https://inews.co.uk/news/science/early-humans-trading-300000-years-135655).

[9] David Orrell and Roman Chlupatý, *The Evolution of Money* (Columbia University Press, 2016).

[10] Adel Daoud, "Scarcity and Artificial Scarcity," *The Wiley Blackwell Encyclopedia of Consumption and Consumer Studies* (24 March 2015).

[11] "Capitalism," *Cambridge Dictionary* online, accessed 17 January 2021 (https://dictionary.cambridge.org/dictionary/english/capitalism?q=Capitalism).

[12] "Exploitation," *Cambridge Dictionary* online, accessed 5 January 2021 (https://dictionary.cambridge.org/us/dictionary/english/exploitation?q=Exploitation).

[13] J.B. Maverick, "How Big Is the Derivatives Market?" *Investopedia*, 30 May 2022 (https://www.investopedia.com/ask/answers/052715/how-big-derivatives-market.asp).

[14] William J. Clinton, "Statement on Signing the Gramm-Leach-Bliley Act," The American Presidency Project, 12 November 1999 (https://www.presidency.ucsb.edu/documents/statement-signing-the-gramm-leach-bliley-act).

[15] Matthias Raddant and Dror Y. Kenett, "Interconnectedness in the Global Financial Market," Office of Financial Research (OFR) Working Paper, 27 September 2016 (https://www.financialresearch.gov/working-papers/files/OFRwp-2016-09_Interconnectedness-in-the-Global-Financial-Market.pdf).

16 Donella Meadows, "Leverage Points: Places to Intervene in a System," Academy for Systems Change, accessed 17 March 2022 (https://donellameadows.org/archives/leverage-points-places-to-intervene-in-a-system/).

17 Meadows, "Leverage Points."

18 Hadas Thier, *A People's Guide to Capitalism: An Introduction to Marxist Economics* (Haymarket Books, 2020).

19 US Department of Housing and Urban Development, "HUD Releases 2020 Annual Homeless Assessment Report Part 1: Homelessness Increasing Even Prior to COVID-19 Pandemic," news release no. 21-041, 18 March 2021 (https://www.hud.gov/press/press_releases_media_advisories/hud_no_21_041).

20 "2020 Population and Housing State Data," United States Census Bureau, 12 August 2021 (https://www.census.gov/library/visualizations/interactive/2020-population-and-housing-state-data.html).

21 "U.S. national health expenditure as percent of GDP 1960 to 2020," Statista, 20 June 2022 (https://www.statista.com/statistics/184968/us-health-expenditure-as-percent-of-gdp-since-1960/).

22 Aria Bendix, "The US was once a leader for healthcare and education—now it ranks 27th in the world," *Business Insider*, 27 September 2018 https://www.businessinsider.com/us-ranks-27th-for-healthcare-and-education-2018-9).

23 Tami Luhby, "US comes in last in health care rankings of high-income countries," *CNN Health*, 4 August 2021 (https://www.cnn.com/2021/08/04/health/us-health-care-rankings/index.html).

24 Paola Zaninotto, George David Batty, Sari Stenholm, Ichiro Kawachi, Martin Hyde, Marcel Goldberg, Hugo Westerlund, Jussi Vahtera, and Jenny Head, "Socioeconomic Inequalities in Disability-free Life Expectancy in Older People from England and the United States: A Cross-national Population-Based Study," *The Journals of Gerontology: Series A* 75, no. 5 (May 2020).

25 Simona Varrella, "Deaths of migrants in the Mediterranean Sea 2014-2021," Statista, 17 September 2021 (https://www.statista.com/statistics/1082077/deaths-of-migrants-in-the-mediterranean-sea/).

26 Hussein A. Amery, "Climate, not conflict, drove many Syrian refugees to Lebanon," *The Conversation*, 3 December 2019 (https://theconversation.com/climate-not-conflict-drove-many-syrian-refugees-to-lebanon-127681).

27 Jennifer Holleis, "How climate change paved the way to war in Syria," *DW*, 26 February 2021 (https://www.dw.com/en/how-climate-change-paved-the-way-to-war-in-syria/a-56711650).

28 James Chen, "Poverty Definition," *Investopedia*, 24 January 2022 (https://www.investopedia.com/terms/p/poverty.asp).

29 John Holmes, "Losing 25,000 to Hunger Every Day," *UN Chronicle*, accessed 15 June 2022 (https://www.un.org/en/chronicle/article/losing-25000-hunger-every-day).

30 "1 in 3 people globally do not have access to safe drinking water – UNICEF, WHO," World Health Organization, 19 June 2019 (https://www.who.int/news/item/18-06-2019-1-in-3-people-globally-do-not-have-access-to-safe-drinking-water-%E2%80%93-unicef-who).

[31] Melissa Denchak, "Water Pollution: Everything You Need to Know," National Resources Defense Council, 18 April 2022 (https://www.nrdc.org/stories/water-pollution-everything-you-need-know).

[32] "Effects of Homelessness on Families and Children," *Issue by Issue*, Institute for Children, Poverty & Homelessness (https://icphusa.org/wp-content/uploads/2015/09/Effects-of-Homelessness.pdf).

[33] Becky Hughes, "Working Homeless Population Grows in Cities across the U.S.," *Parade*, 7 February 2018.

[34] Stephen Eide, *Rust Belt Cities and Their Burden of Legacy Costs*, Manhattan Institute, 24 October 2017 (https://www.manhattan-institute.org/html/rust-belt-cities-and-their-burden-legacy-costs-10729.html).

[35] "Historical Foundations of Race," National Museum of African American History and Culture, Smithsonian, accessed 4 May 2022 (https://nmaahc.si.edu/learn/talking-about-race/topics/historical-foundations-race).

[36] Carter A. Wilson, *Racism: From Slavery to Advanced Capitalism* (Sage Publications, 1996).

[37] "Without Slavery, Would the U.S. Be the Leading Economic Power?" *Here & Now*, WBUR, 19 November 2014 (https://www.wbur.org/hereandnow/2014/11/19/slavery-economy-baptist).

[38] Christian E. Weller, "African Americans Face Systematic Obstacles to Getting Good Jobs," Center for American Progress, 5 December 2019 (https://www.americanprogress.org/article/african-americans-face-systematic-obstacles-getting-good-jobs/).

[39] Olugbenga Ajilore, "3 Ways to Improve the Outcomes for African Americans in the Rural South," Center for American Progress, 6 August 2019 (https://www.americanprogress.org/article/3-ways-improve-outcomes-african-americans-rural-south/).

[40] Howard Gold, "Opinion: The harsh truth about black enrollment at America's elite colleges," MarketWatch, 25 June 2020 (https://www.marketwatch.com/story/the-harsh-truth-about-black-enrollment-at-americas-elite-colleges-2020-06-25).

[41] Anagha Srikanth, "Black people 5 times more likely to be arrested than whites, according to new analysis," *The Hill*, 11 June 2020 (https://thehill.com/changing-america/respect/equality/502277-black-people-5-times-more-likely-to-be-arrested-than-whites).

[42] Christopher Ingraham, "Black men sentenced to more time for committing the exact same crime as a white person, study finds," *The Washington Post*, 16 November 2017 (https://www.washingtonpost.com/news/wonk/wp/2017/11/16/black-men-sentenced-to-more-time-for-committing-the-exact-same-crime-as-a-white-person-study-finds/).

[43] Matt DeRienzo, "Analysis: New and age-old voter suppression tactics at the heart of the 2020 power struggle," The Center for Public Integrity, 28 October 2020 (https://publicintegrity.org/politics/elections/ballotboxbarriers/analysis-voter-suppression-never-went-away-tactics-changed/).

[44] "Infant Mortality and African Americans," US Department of Health and Human Services Office of Minority Health, accessed 4 April 2022 (https://minorityhealth.hhs.gov/omh/browse.aspx?lvl=4&lvlid=23).

[45] Samantha Artiga, Latoya Hill, Kendal Orgera, and Anthony Damico, "Health Coverage by Race and Ethnicity, 2010-2019," Kaiser Family Foundation, 16 July 2021 (https://www.kff.org/racial-equity-and-health-policy/issue-brief/health-coverage-by-race-and-ethnicity/).

[46] Lynette Guastaferro, "Why racial inequities in America's schools are rooted in housing policies of the past," USA Today, 2 November 2020 (https://www.usatoday.com/story/opinion/2020/11/02/how-redlining-still-hurts-black-latino-students-public-schools-column/6083342002/).

[47] Zenitha Prince, "Census Bureau: Higher Percentage of Black Children Live with Single Mothers," The AFRO, 31 December 2016 (https://afro.com/census-bureau-higher-percentage-black-children-live-single-mothers/).

[48] "Incarceration Rates by Country 2022," World Population Review, accessed 2 March 2022 (https://worldpopulationreview.com/country-rankings/incarceration-rates-by-country).

[49] Wendy Sawyer and Peter Wagner, "Mass Incarceration: The Whole Pie 2022," Prison Policy Initiative, 14 March 2022 (https://www.prisonpolicy.org/reports/pie2022.html).

[50] Wesley Rahn, "Alarming level of plastic in children's bodies, German study shows," DW, 14 September 2019 (https://www.dw.com/en/alarming-level-of-plastic-in-childrens-bodies-german-study-shows/a-50432823).

[51] James J. Hoorman and Rafiq Islam, "Understanding Soil Microbes and Nutrient Recycling," Ohioline, 7 September 2010 (https://ohioline.osu.edu/factsheet/SAG-16).

[52] Chris Arsenault, "Only 60 Years of Farming Left If Soil Degradation Continues," Scientific American, 5 December 2014 (https://www.scientificamerican.com/article/only-60-years-of-farming-left-if-soil-degradation-continues/).

[53] Susan Cosier, "The world needs topsoil to grow 95% of its food—but it's rapidly disappearing," The Guardian, 30 May 2019 (https://www.theguardian.com/us-news/2019/may/30/topsoil-farming-agriculture-food-toxic-america).

[54] "Dead zone," National Geographic Society, 20 May 2022 (https://education.nationalgeographic.org/resource/dead-zone).

[55] University of Maryland Center for Environmental Science, "Aquatic 'dead zones' contributing to climate change," ScienceDaily, 12 March 2010 (https://www.sciencedaily.com/releases/2010/03/100311141213.htm).

[56] John Dobberstein, "No-Till, Cover Crop Acres Continue Upward Trend," No-Till Farmer, 10 July 2019 (https://www.no-tillfarmer.com/articles/8929-no-till-cover-crop-acres-continue-upward-trend?v=preview).

[57] Shannon Hall, "Exxon Knew about Climate Change almost 40 years ago," Scientific American, 26 October 2015 (https://www.scientificamerican.com/article/exxon-knew-about-climate-change-almost-40-years-ago/).

[58] "Deforestation," National Geographic Society, 15 July 2022 (https://education.nationalgeographic.org/resource/deforestation).

[59] Renee Cho, "Can Soil Help Combat Climate Change?" State of the Planet, Columbia Climate School, 21 February 2018 (https://news.climate.columbia.edu/2018/02/21/can-soil-help-combat-climate-change/).

[60] Sophie Lewis, "Animal populations worldwide have declined nearly 70% in just 50 years, new report says," *CBS News*, 10 September 2020 (https://www.cbsnews.com/news/endangered-species-animal-population-decline-world-wildlife-fund-new-report/).

[61] "The Most Unexpected Effect of Climate Change," Inter-American Development Bank, accessed 21 April 2022 (https://www.iadb.org/en/improvinglives/most-unexpected-effect-climate-change).

[62] Matthew Sparkes, "Fire at vital tech factory could worsen global computer chip shortage," *New Scientist*, 4 January 2022 (https://www.newscientist.com/article/2303316-fire-at-vital-tech-factory-could-worsen-global-computer-chip-shortage/).

[63] Ximena Del Cerro, "Climate Change Hits Sushi Supply Chain Amid California Water War," *Bloomberg*, 13 August 2021 (https://www.bloomberg.com/news/articles/2021-08-13/climate-change-hits-sushi-supply-chain-amid-california-water-war).

[64] Amy Judd, "B.C. floods: Photos and videos show roads washed away, cars submerged, debris everywhere," *Global News*, 16 November 2021 (https://globalnews.ca/news/8375787/b-c-floods-photos-videos-roads-washed-away-cars-submerged-debris/).

[65] University of Exeter, "Hungry birds as climate change drives food 'mismatch,'" *ScienceDaily*, 23 April 2018 (https://www.sciencedaily.com/releases/2018/04/180423135100.html).

[66] Julia Rosen, "A Billion Sea Creatures Cooked to Death," *The Atlantic*, 4 December 2021 (https://www.theatlantic.com/science/archive/2021/12/extreme-heat-baking-sea-animals-alive/620904/).

[67] Jean-Pierre Gattuso and Lina Hansson, eds., *Ocean Acidification* (Oxford University Press, 2011).

[68] Charles Eisenstein, *The More Beautiful World Our Hearts Know Is Possible* (North Atlantic Books, 2013).

[69] Brian Hare and Vanessa Woods, *Survival of the Friendliest: Understanding Our Origins and Rediscovering Our Common Humanity* (Random House, 2020).

[70] Ted. R. Schultz, "In search of ant ancestors," *PNAS* 97, No. 26, 5 December 2000 (https://www.pnas.org/doi/10.1073/pnas.011513798).

[71] "United States at a Glance," International Wolf Center, accessed 6 June 2022 (https://wolf.org/wow/united-states/).

[72] Emma Bedford, "Number of dogs in the U.S. 2000–2017," Statista, 27 November 2019.

[73] Emma Seppälä, "The Compassionate Mind," *Observer* 26, no. 5, May/June 2013 (https://www.psychologicalscience.org/observer/the-compassionate-mind).

[74] David Graeber, *Bullshit Jobs: A Theory* (Simon and Schuster, 2018).

[75] Nassim Nicholas Taleb, *Antifragile: Things That Gain from Disorder* (Random House, 2012).

[76] "Utopia," *Merriam-Webster.com Dictionary*, accessed 11 May 2022 (https://www.merriam-webster.com/dictionary/utopia).

[77] Jonathan Watts, "Concrete: the most destructive material on Earth," *The Guardian*, 25 February 2019 (https://www.theguardian.com/cities/2019/feb/25/concrete-the-most-destructive-material-on-earth).

[78] Prachi Patel, "Lithium-ion batteries go cobalt free," *Chemical & Engineering News*, 22 July 2020 (https://cen.acs.org/energy/energy-storage-/Lithium-ion-batteries-cobalt-free/98/i29).

[79] Daniel Herriges, "Parking Dominates Our Cities, But Do We Really *See* It?," Strong Towns, 27 November 2019.

[80] "Mapped: All 200 Square Miles of Parking Lot in LA County, as One Giant Parking Lot," Better Institutions, 4 January 2016 (http://www.betterinstitutions.com/blog/2016/1/2/map-a-parking-lot-with-all-of-la-countys-186-million-parking-spaces).

[81] Candelaria Sánchez Galán, "Wind-pumped-hydro Power Station of El Hierro," Fedarene, 2022 (https://fedarene.org/best-practice/wind-pumped-hydro-power-station-of-el-hierro/).

[82] "Cooperative identity, values & principles," International Cooperative Alliance, accessed 15 March 2022 (https://www.ica.coop/en/whats-co-op/co-operative-identity-values-principles).

[83] "Facts and Figures," International Cooperative Alliance, accessed 28 July 2022 (https://www.ica.coop/en/cooperatives/facts-and-figures).

[84] Julie Sloane, "Research Finds Tipping Point for Large-Scale Social Change," Annenberg School for Communication, University of Pennsylvania, 7 June 2018 (https://www.asc.upenn.edu/news-events/news/research-finds-tipping-point-large-scale-social-change).

[85] Daniel H. Pink, *Drive: The Surprising Truth about What Motivates Us* (Riverhead Books, 2009).

[86] *How Millennials Want to Work and Live*, Gallup, 2016 (https://www.gallup.com/workplace/238073/millennials-work-live.aspx).

[87] "World Hunger: Key Facts and Statistics 2022," Action Against Hunger, accessed 19 July 2022 (https://www.actionagainsthunger.org/world-hunger-facts-statistics).

[88] Current World Population, Worldometer, accessed 19 July 2022 (http://srv1.worldometers.info/world-population/).

[89] World Population Milestones, Worldometer, accessed 19 July 2022 (http://srv1.worldometers.info/world-population/).

[90] "Feeding 10 billion people on Earth is possible—and sustainable, scientists say," UChicago News, 4 March 2020 (https://news.uchicago.edu/story/feeding-10-billion-people-earth-possible-and-sustainable-scientists-say).

[91] Isabel V. Sawhill and Christopher Pulliam, "Six facts about wealth in the United States," Brookings Institution, 25 June 2019 (https://www.brookings.edu/blog/up-front/2019/06/25/six-facts-about-wealth-in-the-united-states/).

[92] Peter Joseph, "Economic Calculation in a Natural Law/Resource-Based Economy," The Zeitgeist Movement, Berlin, 3 December 2013 (https://www.youtube.com/watch?v=K9FDIne7M9o).

[93] Victoria Burnett, "A Job and No Mortgage for All in a Spanish Town," *The New York Times*, 26 May 2009.

[94] Caitlin Johnstone, "The Incredible Shrinking Overton Window," Caitlin Johnstone (website), 4 November 2019 (https://caitlinjohnstone.com/2019/11/04/the-incredible-shrinking-overton-window/).

Printed in Great Britain
by Amazon

56417760R00148